A HARD DAY'S SUMMER

ALISON HARGREAVES is a member of the Alpine Club and the elite Alpine Climbing Group. She sits on the International Committee of the British Mountaineering Council and is co-opted onto the Management Committee of the Mount Everest Foundation. Throughout the 1980s and 1990s she has made a bold succession of first British female and first female ascents in the Alps, including a first British female ascent of the Eiger North Face.

She has also climbed in the Himalaya on Lobuche, Lhotse Shar and made a first ascent of the North-West Face of Kantega (6779m).

She has had numerous articles published in the *Alpine Journal*, *High*, *Mountain*, *Mountain Review* and *Vertical* and has appeared in various television features covering the top end of mountaineering as a sport. This is her first book.

A Hard Day's Summer

Six Classic North Faces Solo

Alison Hargreaves

CORONET BOOKS
Hodder and Stoughton

First published in Great Britain in 1994 by Hodder and Stoughton
a division of Hodder Headline PLC
Coronet edition 1995

British Library Cataloguing in Publication Data

Hargreaves, Alison
  Hard Day's Summer: Six Classic North
  Faces Solo
  I. Title
  796.522

ISBN 0 340 64702 7

Printed and bound in Great Britain by
Cox & Wyman Ltd, Reading, Berkshire

Hodder and Stoughton
A division of Hodder Headline PLC
338 Euston Road
London NW1 3BH

This book is dedicated to the family of
Juan Carlos
for the mountain we unknowingly shared.

Contents

A Special Thank-you

'No man is an island' and without help and encouragement from a wide number of people this adventure and hence this book would not ever have happened.

I must first thank my husband, Jim Ballard, for his support and encouragement, both before and throughout the trip, and afterwards in Chamonix, whilst I battled with sheets of paper, for taking the sprogs off on long visits to the woods! Also I thank him for his devotion to climbing literature which produced the historical research.

To my parents, Joyce and John Hargreaves, I am forever grateful for their help and devotion. My father's word processor has been well and truly christened in the many hours of translating my scrawl into some legible typed-up chapters.

A special thank-you to Maggie Body for patiently deciphering and editing the result.

Without the help and friendship of the following this book not have come into being: Steve Aisthorpe; Dick Allen; Sue Ashmore; Erik Bethke; Paula Biner; Bernard Casper; the lads in the Chamonix météo office; John Cleare; Bev England; Olaf Hampe; Bengta, Rike, Hannes and Ernst Hansen-Magnusson; Famke and Gerka Hockstra; Steve and Alex Holland; Martin Johnson; Jaap Leemeijer; Nathalie Monet at the Office de Haute Montagne in Chamonix; Mayke Nagel; Ian Parsons; Dave Peglar; Perkins; Andrea Pickard; Carlton Reid; Piel, Carla, Linda and Marloes Scholten; Robert and Karin Schrott; Hilary Sharp; Dave, Kat, Chloe and Morgan Sharrock; at Sprayway John Hunt, Simon Wright, Annie, Sandy, John, Bill, Keith and Angela; Walter Still; Lars Streblow; Ian (Suds) Sutherland; Ian (Spike) Sykes; Marc Twight; Tom Waghorn; and Ken Wilson.

A big thank-you to everyone, especially those whose names I may have missed.

Alison Hargreaves

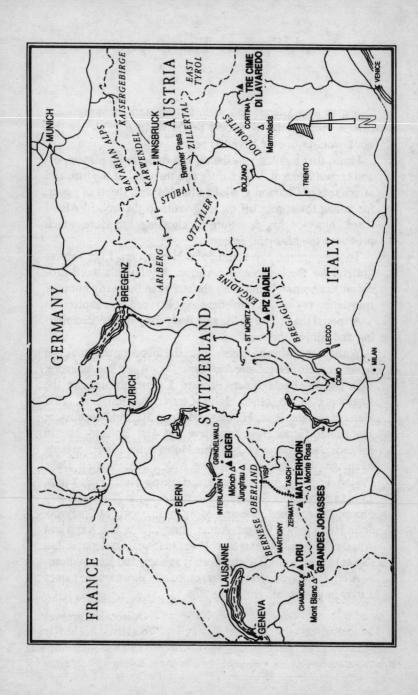

1

THE DREAM
AND THE REALITY

I had never before been alone on a great mixed
face. It was a marvellous and fascinating experience which made me feel freer than ever.

Walter Bonatti

The dream was to spend a whole summer in the Alps along with my
family, Tom aged four and a half, Katie aged two and my husband
Jim (JB). The aim was to travel from area to area climbing a wide
variety of routes to build up the confidence and experience necessary
to undertake my goal of solo climbing a route on each of the six great
classic north faces of the Alps – the Grandes Jorasses, the Matterhorn,
the Eiger, the Piz Badile, the Dru, the Cima Grande – in one season.

The plan was to spend the summer months getting fit so that I could
start the climbs in late winter-early spring 1992–3, an ideal time for
mixed routes, and then finish the last three, which are predominantly
rock, in the early summer, having put in plenty of rock mileage. This
way we would be finished in good time to be gone and away from
popular places such as Chamonix before the high season of August.

In this ideal plan we would be able to spend around a month
enjoying each of the regions we had not visited before, such as the
Bregalia and the Dolomites, getting to know the area and building up
a series of climbs before the hoped-for north face.

The reality was a bit different. It often is. We arrived in the Alps in
March 1993 at the end of a long settled spell of unseasonally mild and
dry weather, and at the beginning of the worst spring and summer for

years. All hopes of peaceful evenings under the stars were shattered with days and nights of rain and wind. Ideas of pleasant summer camping disintegrated with site after site deep in mud. Just everyday existence became hard work, let alone maintaining the motivation to continue my striving for fitness to do the routes.

Due to the late spring snowfalls it was mid-June before I could even consider starting the climbs, and this meant that if I was to achieve all six before a commitment to a trade show in Munich at the beginning of September, we would be able to spend very little time exploring and getting to know the new areas we were to visit.

The only consolation was that because it was mid-June before I was able to start on the Big Six, it meant I had put in three months of solid climbing and training. Consequently my ascents were swift and enjoyable. And as a plus to it all, I was able to complete the whole schedule within an overall record time.

2

NORTH FACES AND UNFINISHED BUSINESS

> The world moves not like an arrow but a boomerang.
>
> Ralph Ellison

Ever since I picked up my first mountain book, *The White Spider* by Heinrich Harrer, as a teenager at school, I have always been fascinated by wild and snowy places. Soon I became more and more engrossed in climbing and its technique, which grew into a deep interest in the Alps and their classic faces.

It was on my first trip to Switzerland ten years ago that I first tried my hand on such a face. At Easter 1983, a good friend, Ian Parsons, and I drove to the huge car park of Täsch, loaded down with provisions for a fortnight, and rode the train up to the twinkling village of Zermatt. Undeterred by the well-meaning elderly ski-tourers suggesting to Ian that it was too dangerous to take young girls into the mountains, we headed up into the Alps on the scenic Gornergrat railway. Donning mountain skis and big rucksacs we started out on a steep descent down a wide gully to the glacier we were going to have to ascend.

My first attempt at ski mountaineering was to prove both educational and knackering! Fresh deep snow on the glacier meant that even the skis were sinking in as we broke trail. I took mine off to make a toilet stop and found myself flipped over and up to my waist in the snow. Refitting my skis, I used my poles to right myself and was ready to go again. I was learning.

We gradually zig-zagged our way through the ever-steepening glacier between huge séracs towards the base of our goal, the great North Face of Liskamm. With the huge bulk of the Monte Rosa massif on our left and the vast expanse of Liskamm stretching to the right, it was an incredible cwm to be in. Our plan was to spend the night on the glacier and then climb a route up the North Face the next day.

With so much fresh snow around, we planned to dig a snow cave for our overnight stop. Working horizontally and then slightly downwards we set about digging our shelter for the night, clad in waterproof tops, bottoms and gloves. Taking it in turns to wield the shovel, I found Ian far more efficient digging at the front end, so soon our technique as we got deeper was for Ian to dig and me to scrabble the snow back and out behind us like an eager mole. Before long we had a warm and sheltered home and set about preparing luxuries such as thin insulating mats and down sleeping bags kept dry in caterpillar-like Gore-Tex bivouac bags. Food and drink were next on the priority list. Out came the Gaz stove, we filled the billie with snow from the cave walls and melted it. Shelves were unnecessary as we could poke spoons and knives into the icy walls, and all our climbing equipment could be suspended from ice screws. Our skis stood up at the entrance, so that if we got blocked in during the night with a heavy snowfall, at least someone out there would know where we were buried! Or so we fondly imagined.

As the stove hummed away I lay snug in all my clothes – down jacket, waterproofs, hat, gloves – inside my sleeping bag. I smiled and felt calm. Simplicity in itself was my happiness.

During the night I woke to the howling wind outside. Using spare overtrousers and rucsacs, we blocked up the entrance, backing them up with ice axes to prevent the continual blast of cold spindrift from getting in round the edges. Presumably this storm was the reason yesterday's ski-tourers were heading rapidly off the mountain, pointing to the appearing clouds and muttering something about a south wind, as we had been merrily plodding slowly upwards. The tell-tale mackerel clouds and south winds, which I have since learnt to respect, meant bad weather imminent in under twenty-four hours. The skiers were speeding back down, while we had been heading up to experience it!

Breakfast – and it was time to move. Daylight, or almost, but where were our skis? Last night they had stuck at least four feet out of the snow, now there was no sign of them! With everything packed into our rucksacs and wearing all our spare clothes, we dug around until we finally found our skis. With so much fresh snow and huge avalanche trains rumbling down, the North Face of Liskamm was no place to be that morning so we headed back down.

Unaccustomed to skiing, let alone downhill with a huge rucksac, I had to develop my own technique for keeping my speed under control. Although the ski-tourers around blasted down the short but steep plug at the base of the glacier in a series of quick neat turns to arrive at the flat pistes underneath, I carefully side-slipped my way to the bottom, pointing my ski tips inward to snow plough and retard my progress, to the annoyance of the impatient skiers.

Back in Zermatt we met up briefly with Ian's friend Jim Fotheringham and his partner to ask how they had got on with their attempt on the North Face of the Matterhorn. Like us they had been driven down by the weather, but said conditions on the face had been good. Now they were heading off to find consolation in a few days' piste skiing. So Ian and I decided to head up to the Hörnli Hut for an attempt on the North Face of the Matterhorn ourselves.

After an exhausting day's climb direct through the rock ridge, after losing the deep snow-covered path, we finally arrived at the huge and splendidly situated Hörnli Hotel and Hut. Both were closed. But out of season, when the hut is not under the care of a guardian, the winter room is kept open for climbers. So we used the metal ladder at the side to climb through an upstairs window into the dark and eerie winter refuge.

I took off my leather double boots, only to be lumbered with an agonising pain in one heel which had been broken in an accident years before. My new touring boots had rubbed in just the wrong place. Ian finally found some painkillers in the first-aid cabinet, and life was bearable.

But the weather conditions were not to change. We finally headed down, privileged to have been on the mountain, but with unfinished business to return to.

That autumn of 1983 my fascination with north faces was to continue. I climbed my first Alpine route, the North Face of the Aiguille du Midi via the Frendo Spur. The North Face of the Tour Ronde was next and the last ten days in glorious weather were spent on new and classic rock climbs. The end of the following May saw Ian

Parsons and me at the Hörnli Hut once more, with the renewed intention of attempting the North Face. However, huge falls of snow and bad weather again thwarted our efforts.

We drove back to Chamonix and were about to continue home, when we glanced at the promising weather report from the top station of the Aiguille du Midi téléphérique. It meant we were able to climb a major route after all, the Super Couloir on Mont Blanc du Tacul.

In June '84 and back in Chamonix, again with Ian, we warmed up on the Vaucher route on the Aiguille du Peigne and then walked up into the fantastic glacial cirque of the Argentière Basin. In the early hours of the following morning we set off from the Argentière Hut, crossing the glacier, now frozen hard after the night's frost, and continued to the base of the North Face of Les Courtes. We climbed the Swiss route and descended by the North-east Couloir, carefully down-climbing to the glacier which had turned from grey to soggy pink as we plodded back to the hut.

The next day we were off again, before dawn, with headlamp torches up the now refrozen glacier. At the bergschrund we donned crampons, roped up and set about climbing the North Face of the Triolet. What we hoped would be an easier proposition than the previous day's climb proved much harder and more serious. The ice was black, hard and uncompromising. Each placement of a pick shattered the ice and sometimes needed a couple of swings to get a secure hold. It was to be exhausting climb, but we made it.

After a long and complicated glacier descent down the west side to the Couvercle Hut, and so to the valley, we went out to celebrate in style. Ian met an old friend from New Zealand and their reunion went on into the night. Tired and unsettled I left early. The weather was still good, we were fit, we still had time . . .

A call to Frau Paula Biner at the Hotel Bahnhof in Zermatt rewarded us with an encouraging response. The guides would be climbing the classic Hörnli Ridge for the first time that year the next day, she told us. Conditions on the Matterhorn looked good.

With great enthusiasm we piled into the car. With Ian looking worse for wear, I drove to Switzerland and the car park at Täsch. As promised the next day dawned clear at the Hörnli Hut and we were already high on the icefield as dawn appeared, to enjoy a wondrous sunrise. It was late afternoon as we made the summit. The intense pleasure of that moment reached right to the core. However, from the summit ridge, there is still 1700 metres of awkward down-climbing to the Hörnli Hut, and it was getting late. We could not linger, and set off down. Tired after a hectic few days, I grasped the large fixed ropes on the initial steep rocky section tightly before the ground became more broken and not so intimidating. Night overtook us and we had not found the Solvay emergency bivouac hut, a tiny wooden shack with enough sleeping room for eight people and a radio telephone for emergencies. We lay down on the next rocky ledge that we could find. Tired, thirsty and hungry, I climbed into my paper bivvy bag, made from the material builders use for temporary covering, and fell into a deep exhausted sleep. Poor Ian had no bivvy bag however and to add insult to injury the constant crackling of mine kept him awake all night. Whilst I was annoyed to be woken next morning by the season's first party of guides and clients up the Hörnli Ridge, Ian was glad to be able to move and get warm. We could not expect any congratulations or pleasantries from the Swiss guide, presumably, like myself, not too good first thing in the morning and not pleased at two Brits climbing 'his' mountain by the North Face without the benefit of his professional services. His response was that his son could have climbed it far quicker! So, warmed by his greeting, we set off down.

The hut guardian was pleasanter but surprised! We continued down to Schwarzsee to be in the sun beside its beautiful water on lush flower-scented banks in what was now a fantastic summer afternoon. All too quickly it was time to descend to Zermatt and have my first taste of the warmth, friendship and generosity of Frau Paula Biner at the Hotel Bahnhof. Her famous guide brother Bernard has been the host and friend to many climbers, especially the English. When he died Paula continued his role. Her congratulations turned into afternoon tea, which we humbly enjoyed.

So finally, I had climbed that beautiful mountain, the Matterhorn – and my appetite was whetted. I still had many more to climb. It was autumn 1985 before I was back in the Alps again and pursuing my fascination with north faces. This time it was the Grandes Jorasses. After acclimatising on the Chère Couloir, Mont Blanc du Tacul, Ian Parsons and I focused our energies into an autumnal ascent up the magnificent line of the Croz Spur.

Two Himalayan expeditions later – Kangtega, Lobuche, Lhotse Shar and Ama Dablam – and the autumn of 1987 saw me back again at the base of the Grandes Jorasses. After being thwarted by bad weather on the North Face of the Eiger, Phil Dickens and I sped round to Chamonix in the hope of a climb before the start of a film shoot I was committed to in a couple of days.

With a promise of 'beau temps' we raced up the Mer de Glace and settled ourselves in the Leschaux Hut for the evening. An early start and we were soon at the top of that wonderful ice climb of the Shroud in excellent conditions, and back at Montenvers Station by evening.

It is only the very fortunate (or under-ambitious) climber who ends a season in the Alps with no unfinished business. Mine in 1987 was with the Eiger, so I was back the following summer with Steve Aisthorpe for a fiftieth anniversary ascent of the original 1938 route on the Eigerwand. I was the first British woman to climb the North Face and I could claim another record, too. For by now I was married to Jim Ballard and when I climbed the Eiger I was five and a half months pregnant. Tom was born in October.

By the following autumn of 1989 Tom was growing well and I was back to my great north faces. Steve Aisthorpe and I climbed the face which dominates the Argentière Glacier basin, Les Droites. A cold and wintry ascent of the Corneau-Davaille with the Shea-Jackson finish. The mountain had been cold, the days short and the summit descent awkward. I wondered if my obsession with north faces had run its course. With some great climbs and wonderful mountains under my belt, thoughts turned to warm rock and sunny days. And yet those north faces would not be dislodged from my dreams.

Our second child, Kate, was born in 1991 and as she grew up I once more felt the urge to begin climbing again. When the children were babies it was hard to plan ahead and we began to go out more as a family to local outcrops at evenings and weekends. This was how I began to boulder seriously and from there developed to attempting solo climbs of greater height and difficulty. Splendid summer afternoons on Peak and Yorkshire gritstone increased my fitness and confidence. So did days in Wales, based at my parents' cottage at Penmaenmawr, ticking off fine classic climbs I had never had the chance to do before.

I found that solo climbing seemed to suit me. It needed that total commitment that I had not always been prepared to make before. The overall satisfaction was something I had not previously experienced. To be at one and in tune with the rock and its features was engrossing and stimulating. Not only that, but I was able to revel in moving fast and efficiently. I have never been a very patient climbing partner.

As the routes piled up, so did my ambitions, and new horizons and ideas appeared. Why not extend my newfound skills to the Alps?

In March 1992 I drove myself to Chamonix to try my hand at solo winter Alpine climbing. With a clutch of climbs under my solo belt – the Jager Couloir and the Mazeaud Contamine, both on Mont Blanc du Tacul, and the 'Y' Couloir on the Aiguille d'Argentière – I felt fit and acclimatised. Time for the Matterhorn!

However the icefield was very brittle and conditions generally bad, so I decided to content myself with climbing the Hörnli Ridge. After five and a half hours and passing several roped teams, I was on that wonderful lofty summit.

The plan was for a speedy descent and a hot supper at the hut! However this was not to be. Some of the climbers whom I had passed had now turned back, realising that the summit was out of their reach. But without a long rope they were finding it increasingly hard to descend, so I found myself involved in helping shepherd five of them down through a drawn-out descent involving a long cold night.

It was the middle of the next morning before I felt able to leave them at the top of the last easy section, and chased down to the hut. Then, looking at my feet, I discovered sure signs of frostbite in several toes. The hospital in Chamonix where I went to check out the damage suggested no Alpine climbing for a minimum of twelve months! Horrified, I returned home after good treatment, pleased with the way things had worked out, but with some *very* unfinished business . . .

3

ALPINE MONSOONS

Swallows and Amazons for ever!

Nancy Blackett

The end of March 1993 and almost ten years since my first Alpine season, we were back in sunny Chamonix. We had hoped and planned to be there by the end of February at the latest, giving me long enough to tune my fitness and acclimatise and be able to climb one of the Big Six before 21st March, the end of the winter season.

However, the reality meant it was near the end of March before the odds and ends were tidied up and we could finally get underway. The late morning of the 22nd and we finally loaded up Perkins the Land-Rover with gear and equipment. We had managed to buy some large blue plastic industrial chemical barrels which, after scrubbing out, fitted perfectly laid sideways on the roof rack. Two days of packing, labelling and listing with my parents and all the seventeen barrels were ready. With the help of my dad I had removed the forward rear seats, leaving a well, and fitted large wooden shelves under the rear bench seats to widen them, for both sleeping and the child safety seats. After hours of frustration and fiddling JB managed to fit inertia seat belts to secure them. Kitted out with remnants of spare carpet, and with an extra rug on top for luxury, Perkins was turned into a home. All that remained was to pack the plastic boxes of maps and guide books inside, the plastic stacking boxes of cutlery, cooking pots, stoves, fuel and condiments, load in pillows, sleeping bags, mats, and we could go. But not before we had weighed ourselves down with huge linen Cairngorm rope bags full of books and armfuls of favourite soft toys for the children. With tears and waves we set off down my parents' steep drive and so to the road south.

Two days of steady driving through rural France and after a second overnight stop in the Jura, we dropped down to Geneva and took the road up the valley to Chamonix. Taking on board a hypermarket's worth of food en route, we set about sorting out a suitable base for the next few weeks.

We decided that, as the nights were still cold and the weather forecast mixed, to make life easier for us all, we would hire a caravan for the first week. The settled dry winter weather was drawing to a close, as unfortunately we were about to find out!

That first week we settled into a kind of routine quite quickly. Kate would wake us promptly at seven and Jim would put on the porridge for breakfast and then fry eggs. We made regular pilgrimages to the météo station in Chamonix, but the long-term weather reports were barely encouraging. When we woke to a blanket of snow the best way to wear out Tom and Kate was to take them sledging halfway up Les Bossons piste. It was good exercise, I told myself, pulling two sprogs uphill on a sledge.

On the days when we had some clearer weather, we sorted out the gear and drove down the valley to Les Houches for some easy cragging to help loosen up on rock which was cold but dry. Another day we took a look at the Col des Montets but it was still very snowy, so we headed back up the valley to a crag at La Joux. While the children played happily at the bottom, I got in five routes before the sun went down. I realised however that with this big late fall of fresh snow the higher climbs were going to be out of the question. So I continued to keep active in the valley while the mountains warmed up and the snow melted.

Sunday, 28th March was Kate's second birthday and a glorious spring day, so we drove down to Le Fayet for a change of rock. JB took the sprogs to a lovely park where they played for nearly three hours among the local children and Kate managed to lose yet another pair of sunglasses. When we got back she reliably informed us that she had put them in the litter bin!

After a family picnic lunch we headed back towards Chamonix via Servoz. But after thrashing through the Sunday crowds I needed a break, so we returned to the campsite and I went in search of some stamina exercise. Running up a steep hill I ground to a halt when faced by deep snow at around 1900 metres, but the compensation was fantastic views over Mont Blanc. Weary and rejuvenated I descended for a birthday tea and for Kate's attempt to blow out the candles. She really loved us all singing 'Happy birthday to you'.

Our week in the caravan site was running out now and JB was keen to move on, but there were only two designated campsites open yet in the valley, which didn't give us much choice. An alternative would have been to move to another area and return when conditions improved. But my vision was already tunnelled. I had six big routes and faces to climb, two of which were here, and I was not easily to be dragged away. I felt really reluctant to leave until I had one at least under my belt. I just wanted to sit tight until the approaches to the routes improved somewhat. Also I felt a lot happier knowing the children had a nice safe base to enjoy.

So we stayed put and went out for more day jaunts to Les Gaillands and, for another change of scenery, we drove to Servoz and I got in a lot of mileage perfecting my back-roping technique with a new device I had been sent from America called a Soloist. I could protect myself with this by means of a back rope and so was able to get fitter tackling harder rock climbs in the valley. I had hopes this device would also stand me in good stead on some sections of the Big Six.

Each day I wondered about the chance to make a start on one of these, but the météo was disappointing for setting out on a big sustained climb. Instead we continued to make do with cragging. Our favourite was Le Joux. We would park by the railway line and Tom would run off and up through the meadows to find the little track that wound its way up through the trees to the crag. He and Kate had plenty to amuse them while I happily ticked off the routes.

April Fool's Day was the day we were going to give up caravan luxury and start camping in earnest. Although it felt like a wasted effort at the time, I had to repack everything into the barrels and load it all on to Perkins so that we could make our move – 100 yards up the hill! By 11.30 a.m. I had emptied everything and cleaned out the van, while JB had gone ahead to find the best spot to pitch our tents. Now he drove Perkins up to the site, loaded loosely with barrels and boxes and we set about establishing our new home. Because our movements this summer needed to be flexible to take advantage of good weather slots in different parts of the Alps, we could never prebook fixed accommodation, so camping was to be our lot. Camping with children, I decided, is definitely more tiring and takes more planning than organising an expedition.

I was determined, however, to retain some normal creature comforts. Our bedding was an example of this! Layers of thick insulated mats, then inflatable mattresses, layers of spare sleeping bags covered in underblankets and then a sheet formed the base and with crisp sheets and our own down quilts on top, our nests were topped off by the softest of our down pillows.

Tom generally felt grown up and preferred to have his own tent which, after he'd thrown in all his bags of Lego, soft toys and cars, looked like the usual boy's bedroom. Kate however was still small and, whilst we tried her in her own little 'room', after a few nights of retrieving her, undressed and in the depths of darkness, JB decided that life would be easier if she remained permanently in with us. Fortunately our big tent had a fine bell end, which made the perfect miniature room for a wee one.

In the night the rain turned to snow. The forecast was for more, and no good weather for days. The météo told us the whole of the South of France was also having wet weather, so it wasn't going to be worth going down there either. Anyway the tents were too wet to move.

To camp well and comfortably in the rain needs good planning and organisation; to camp well in the rain with two young children needs even more planning, plus a lot more perseverance. Ours was going to be tried to the extreme. Confined to the back of a Land-Rover for mealtimes with two active sprogs was not easy for someone with my short fuse. We made snowmen and paid another visit to the météo men to be depressed.

Next morning we went for a family walk down to the base of the Bossons Glacier which for many years had been a popular place for a spot of accessible ice-climbing, but it had been eleven years since I was last there and it had receded by an amazingly huge distance. No longer did it curve down and along the horizontal section of a valley it had carved out for itself. Now it disappeared way back up the boulder-strewn hillside behind. Not a sensible place for the sprogs, so we zig-zagged back down the path to Les Bossons. JB, who had taken over cooking and kitchen duties, prepared a fine lunch of cooked vegetarian burger sarnies. As non-meat-eaters we were very grateful to have been supplied for the whole of the summer with a wide variety of dehydrated foods, distributed by a vegetarian food company called Haldane. These kept us well fed and unfed-up with their range throughout the whole summer. Quite a tribute! And over the weeks

JB became a dab hand at preparing burgers and sausages from the dehydrated mixes. Their cheese and onion sausage mix became a favourite with us all!

All our hopes of pleasant spring camping were being rapidly washed away as the weather deteriorated from bad to worse and our home was being turned into more of a paddy field than a campsite. I was not able to get any mountain routes done and conditions continued to make life exceptionally hard work, as my diary records:

MONDAY 5TH APRIL

A most beautiful cold, clear, crisp night, after a very heavy quick fall of snow, so there was a beautiful white crust of sugar on everything. *Freezing* cold. I decided to dress the sprogs *inside* the tent. It would be nice just to slip on slippers and get up for breakfast, but here it means boots, Polartec and Gore-Tex even to get up for the loo! It was too cold to eat outside, so JB cautiously passed the porridge in to us. I took Kate down to the drying room with me to collect yesterday's washing and to warm her through, then returned to clear snow from the tents before the sun hit and started to melt everything. In my enthusiasm I ripped a panel on the store tent. So after emptying and drying it, JB had to mend it, before the next lot of bad weather.

The mountains looked beautiful, snowy and sunny. Lots and lots of fresh snow to plough through, but beautifully plastered.

After lunch we took photos in the woods and then a trip to Les Gaillands, where I discovered some dried rock and was able to cover some meterage.

A welcome break in this pattern of bad weather, when the sun comes out it's powerful and hot on our backs, quite a pleasant change!

TUESDAY 6TH APRIL

Oh dear, rain all night and rain all day. This morning there were oddments of shopping to do in town but this afternoon, after a look at the météo, we resorted to the swimming baths in Chamonix.

WEDNESDAY 7TH APRIL

Rain, rain, rain . . . it's not stopped again all day today. After my stint of Lego-minding with the sprogs, I head off for a run. Taking a path across the river and on to the slopes of the Aiguilles Rouges I started to work uphill, following a steep path zig-zagging up through the trees. All the recent wet snow had created havoc in the woods. Another 1.4 metres of fresh snow has fallen higher up. Huge avalanche danger. Everywhere in Chamonix there were notices warning ski-tourers against going into the mountains in such conditions. With only bad weather approaching I have finally decided to call it a day. The time has come to move on somewhere else. Reluctantly, we have to pack up and move south.

We were aiming for the Alpes Maritimes and some rock climbing. So all aboard Perkins, who became home and transport once again. Using wooden wedges I was able to tilt the bench seat cushions to a reasonable angle so the children could lie and sleep without sliding off – whatever the tilt on the Land-Rover. Then getting out pillows and sleeping bags – which we always kept handy for journeys – I changed them into pyjamas before snuggling them down with an armful of soft toys for the night. As we had removed the two back seats, we were able to fill the well with plastic boxes of goodies in constant use – a box of cutlery and crockery, another of sugar, coffee, jam, dilutable drink, salt. On the other side was a box of guide books and maps covering any area of Europe that we might require throughout the summer, and on top of that a box of paperwork – files on sponsors, routes, pads of paper, and for the sprogs, diaries, pencils, pens and a huge pencil sharpener, strongly recommended for a long-term trip with children.

These boxes were easily accessed by the side doors, and made Perkins into a bedroom/kitchen/office – all rolled into one! The cool box (which proved brilliant) slotted in between the two side seats and, come night, was easily lifted out so that I could lay out an inflatable mattress on the floor and get a comfortable night's rest.

If the weather was bad JB would sleep across the front seats, leaving a door ajar for full extension; but on clear, starry nights he slept out and watched over us from outside.

Perkins was not only our transport – he was our home. The children took to him like a friend and we came to rely upon and use him for almost everything. So it was like an illness in the family when at 8.30 a.m. on Good Friday morning we shredded a tyre on the side of a steep hairpin bend; with a heavily laden Land-Rover this was a touch exciting! We limped down to Gap where we had to invest in two new tyres as they were unable to match any we had in use, and we found a magnificent plastic tractor for Katie's late birthday present. So everyone's transport was sorted out and we could move on.

Our next port of call was the tiny village of St Martin-Vesubie, with a promise of sun-baked Alpine rock and snakes for company. The idea of a couple of weeks' mountain rock climbing greatly appealed after the weather we had experienced. However, after a long tiring drive, we arrived to be informed that the local hut guardians had not managed to open yet. They had been turned back trying to ski in through chest-deep snow. 'Yes, it was very unusual,' everyone agreed. We decided to continue south as far as we could, to the Côte d'Azur, then turn right and keep going to the magical area of perfect weather, wonderful limestone and scenery known as Les Calanques. We might be moving further and further away from the Alps, but at least there the weather would not be able to stop me putting in some serious training climbs.

4

GETTING IN GEAR IN LES CALANQUES AND LES ECRINS

Now Voyager sail forth to seek and find.
Walt Whitman

Our journey to the coast was to prove a wise move. Here I was able to complete day upon day of long approaches to wild areas and to climb wonderful routes at my leisure. Warm sunny days after the cold and rain rejuvenated my enthusiasm, even though we were far from the mountains I had come to climb.

I could rock climb, prepare and dream. We combined coastal family cragging days with long mountainous wilderness days and whilst JB and the children amused themselves on the coast, I went off on long approaches for some of the great classic climbs. Great high rocky ridges rising out of the sea, and long limestone arêtes bursting out of wild mountain valleys made for spectacular and enjoyable climbing.

At last the sun was hot and the children could swap fleece for shorts and sandals while they played happily in the rocky coves with their steep limestone walls above deep blue sea. As for me, I had a famous world at my fingertips and Gaston Rébuffat's hefty *100 Best Routes in the Calanques* weighed down my knee in the evenings. The climbing at En Vau's rocky towers and walls is arguably some of the best, if overcrowded. I followed an arête up a series of pinnacles and savoured the grand situation as I waited for two teams ahead to move off, before motoring to the top. But it was perfectly possible to escape the crowds. Another day I did the Arête Intégrale du Cloportes and had the privilege of watching a pair of eagles playing in the air currents. I thought how good it was to be able to expand the children's natural history awareness on this trip with the sight of chamoix and marmots in the remoter places we visited. One morning I was proud to find Tom inside his tent very gently studying a beautiful little spider.

I ticked off the Arête des Huit Gendarmes, Castelveil, the Voie de la Calanque, the Paillon on the Grande Aiguille and the Pouce Normal. I could feel myself building up my fitness every day as I got a proper training programme under way. By the end of our visit to the Calanques I should have over 3000 metres of rock routes under my belt and many more metres of ascent.

We travelled further west and I scrambled through scrubby slopes to climb on hot white south-facing rock. Bolted climbing has brought many more routes and many more climbers to the south faces of the classic ridges of Les Lames and the Rocher des Goudes, but I managed to avoid both bolts and bolters with some blissful hours of solitude, ending on the Arête de la Cordée, a great classic line that completes the ridge from the Col de Lune to the summit. As I sat there appreciating the panorama I received some surprised 'Bonjour's from two heavy teams who had come up from St Michel's South Face. Then I traced a way across the top to find a narrow path descending past ancient caves. I paused to watch the antics of some hot rock jocks on the roof of one impressively overhung cave while a hidden guitarist strummed from the depths and whiffs of music pursued me downwards.

Sormiou became a favourite place. The sand was delightful and the bathing shallow, so perfectly safe for the children, while over the Col de Sormiou even Tom managed some bolted routes in bare feet and shorts. As for me, I exchanged trainers for rock shoes, donned my chalk bag and was off up the Tour de l'Extrême Bec par Bord de la Mer. Various parties in front of me had started the traverse leftwards; all but one had gone upwards after a short way on to another route, rather than continue the fine traverse, just above the lapping of the sea, to the far extremity at the nose. The rock was great, the situation fine. I waved to a team of passing divers in a boat heading out to sea, and started on up the arête of the nose. After sixty metres the climbing eased back into a scrambly rocky ridge, and after a lunch stop to watch the birds and the sea, I carried on up the Arête de Sormiou northwards before descending just west of the coastal car parks. The sprogs were ecstatic – the sand was soft, the sea was warm, they'd found a bucket and some sand moulds and were having a whale of a time.

The only member of the party who wasn't enjoying himself was Perkins. We had thrashed him unladen up and over cols for long enough. Now he would have no more of it. As we ground up the last steep bit towards the top of the Col de Sormiou yet again, one morning something in his gear box went and he could no longer perform. Fortunately we were on the right side of the col, but unfortunately it was too narrow to turn round, so we had to roll gently and steeply backwards until JB managed to negotiate into a layby and swing round. The damage? Perkins no longer had a first gear and just to make matters worse, he had no reverse either. JB experimented with the gear box and discovered that by using second, four-wheel and overdrive the invalid was still quite manageable, but I wondered for how long. To make matters worse, we found when we got back to camp in Cassis that someone had been through our tents and taken our English and Swiss currency which I had forgotten to transfer to my waistbag. On top of that it started to rain again. 'The worst spring in thirty years,' the locals lamented miserably. Tom and Kate were digging water channels with their spades.

I called in at the garage for a medical report on Perkins. Things looked bleak. There was no cheap second-hand gear box to be had locally. To have one sent out from the UK would be a slow job, to have one sent fast would be an expensive job. Perkins might tick over for another thirty years, or he might not make it back to the campsite. We decided to wait until it stopped raining and give Perkins a whirl. April ended and May began and I still hadn't climbed one of the Big Six. On 3rd May we set off back to the mountains.

The campsite nearest Les Ecrins was officially closed but a friendly chap from the National Park assured us that it would be okay. It was a delightful spot beside the river and Tom and Kate were soon happily digging in the sand and collecting pine cones from the woods behind us. We were in an area near Briançon which boasted 300 sunny days out of the 365 in its tourist literature. All we had to do, said JB, was sit out the first 65 in that case and all would be well.

My diary records my pleasure at my first Alpine route of the season:

WEDNESDAY 5TH MAY

Walked steeply to the tiny beautiful mountain hamlet of L'Alpe du Lauzet and headed into the snowline alongside the Torrent du Rif. Plodding slowly across a peaceful snow slope in hot sun, sinking deep at every step. Suddenly there was a loud shrieking in front of me and a marmot appeared through the snow. Then another, and another. They proceeded to loll around in the sun for a while before having a brisk run round to stretch their legs. Were they coming out of hibernation? As there were no other tracks around I assumed so. Later I saw lots and lots appearing all over the virgin white slopes. Popping their noses through first, then slowly climbing out and rolling in contentment. I felt very honoured.

In deep snow I continued up to the lofty viewpoint on Col des Ponsonnières and proceeded to climb my first Alpine route of the year – the Arête de la Bruyère, a wonderful pinnacled knife-edge ridge. While it's presumably a pleasant classic rock route in warm summer weather, I enjoyed great winter conditions. It was too snowy to wear rock boots and so I climbed in my favourite Brasher boots and before long was engrossed in my situation. A tricky descent in wet sun-warmed snow, grinning happily to myself as I passed yet more furry fellows basking in the afternoon sun. Sat to wring out my socks after crossing the swollen river by a lovely hand-hewn wooden trough, with a warm glow inside I started the long descent back down the valley to Le Casset and the family. In a great area on a beautiful day. What more could I have asked for?

But the good weather didn't last. Soon it was as misty and damp and depressing as it had ever been. Concerned about the dangers of avalanches, I tested out the snow up the Couloir Davin and in my descent under the Pics du Casset I had to fight my way, often in snow waist deep, lying horizontal in places to avoid being sucked in further. Doom and gloom. The weather and the mountains were really getting the better of me. But the next day on a family walk up the Tabuc the children were thrilled to see the marmots and hear them chuntering, and as we descended through the trees we spotted roaming chamoix and crossed a grassy alp covered in the loveliest wildflowers.

A Hard Day's Summer

Headed up from Pont d'Alpe to the base of the Aiguillette Lauzet. By now it was snowing. The rock was wet and the cloud low. I decided to continue straight on up the couloir right of the Aiguille and so to Point 2717m. Not finding a reasonable way (in fact it was desperate!), I continued traversing north on the assumption I would find the via ferrata to the summit. However, after traversing hideous snowy slopes I had had enough. No via ferrata. I headed straight up through a desperate rock band, gripped when one of my only two holds broke. I raced up like a startled rabbit and broke through the cornice with very cold hands to the narrow summit ridge.

Only to discover that I was no longer on my own but surrounded by four huge tents, aerials all over the place, and a dozen people, all dressed in white, carefully sheltering in dug-out igloo shelters!

They were going to be joined by 15,000 soldiers who were exercising in the area for the next couple of weeks. As I descended to the valley I discovered that the children had spent all day watching trucks, jeeps, light tanks and ambulances that had been to collect the soldiers who had force-marched over the Col d'Arsine. We sat in the rain and watched helicopter after helicopter. The next few days were to prove entertaining. Walks were diverted by 'MINE' signs on paths, and regularly a gun with a soldier fastened to it would pop up from behind boulders. We were informed by an English-speaking officer who had just returned from liaison with the Americans in Somalia that the exercise involved troops of all calibre . . .

The middle of May and the wind had changed direction. We wondered if this was what we had been waiting for. On Monday 17th May I arrived at Col des Près les Fonts (3221m) after climbing the fine Couloir Davin, my first snow and ice route of this trip and my highest point so far. Well chuffed, I descended in beautiful weather through deep porridge-like snow to a beautiful hanging valley, with chamoix and thousand upon thousand of wonderful gentians and white poppies. A couple of days of rain and damp rock followed that and then we were all set to move on until . . .

THURSDAY 20TH MAY

Oh dear! What a day! JB woke at 7.30 a.m. and went to our makeshift kitchen to put water for porridge on the MSR stove only to find the stove and billies missing.

Then he went to look at the packed barrels, ready for our move today. Some missing? I counted them and could not find my climbing gear. Shock-horror, the two barrels of our climbing gear were gone. The English-speaking lad we had served tea to last night, who was supposedly meeting his mate, was gone too. According to one of the British Army team cycling from Italy to Aldershot for charity who were camping further up the site, he had disappeared very fast down the valley in the early hours of the morning.

I found it so hard to believe, I kept counting the barrels over again in case I couldn't add up. I think the thing that I found hardest was the fact that I'd misjudged him. I'd totally got him wrong and I lost all my self-confidence in trusting anyone.

When we'd returned from a wet afternoon at the local park I was surprised and annoyed to find a fancy car parked *right* on our little plot of land. Why with so much space around should anyone want to invade someone else's privacy quite so much, I'd thought. Then as we jumped out of Perkins this tall lad with a springer spaniel came and introduced himself. His tale was that he was supposed to meet some people here, a chap with a young family; they had similar tents to ours, and he thought it was us. He'd had all his equipment stolen and was returning back to Scotland after a winter instructing in Spain (he was as brown as a berry). He was to swop ideas with this mate who was travelling down from the UK to take over his post in Spain. On the face of it he had seemed an okay sort of chap, a touch odd, but no more than that. He'd been chatty and interested in us and our trip, and we'd talked about the area, its beauty, peacefulness and the lack of tourists. The back quarter light of his car was broken, we noticed. By the thieves who had stolen all his outdoor kit, he'd explained. Of course we only realised later that it was *he* who had been the break-in culprit when stealing the car!

So gearless, and without tent and stove, we'd taken pity on him and made him cups of tea. He had chatted to the sprogs, and even offered to babysit for us, should we want a night out, saying he understood how difficult it was for parents away with young children to get a break. I shudder to think what might have happened had we taken up his offer and gone out. Not only more gear stolen, but perhaps the children, if not taken away, certainly abandoned. Presumably while we were out in the afternoon he had gone through our barrels, with the excuse that he thought they belonged to his mate, should he be confronted, and so discovered which he thought the most worth stealing. Then, having waited till all were asleep, he had carefully removed the two he'd earmarked and zoomed away at breakneck speed.

I was upset. I was grateful to think that at least we'd not been stupid enough to trust him with the children, but it had obviously left a mark on them anyway. At the same time as we discovered the barrel loss, Katie's soft rabbit went missing too and she was convinced 'the nasty man' took it. It concerned me that the children had been exposed to theft so early, but at least I hoped that the awareness of its consequences would act as a future deterrent in their own cases.

So now we had a poorly Perkins, no climbing gear and yet again it was throwing it down – and not one of the Big Six to show for our time and trouble.

Our plan had been to drive round into the heart of Les Ecrins and explore and climb from there. So although we were over-damped by the weather and circumstances (form-filling with the Gendarmerie), we travelled round into the secluded valley of Ailefroide. On our arrival we were warned by two young English climbers to be on our guard, as two days before a tall slim English lad had tried to break into their car whilst they were up on the hills!

We climbed on the handy valley crags, and made camp fires with the plentiful supply of dead wood. The luxury of copious amounts of *hot* water! The children enjoyed the camp fires. The weather was not vastly better, but the days of rain got less and it generally just turned into unsettled, usually dry mornings and rain in the afternoons. Fortunately, I had left an axe and a pair of crampons drying out in Perkins.

SUNDAY 23RD MAY

Up around 6.00 a.m., light and bright. By 7.25 a.m. I was walking up through the wooded valley to the Cézanne Hut. Behind the hut I came across a tame chamois foraging for scraps, and a hundred yards further on a fine marmot was momentarily nonplussed when he got himself caught between me and a couple descending in the opposite direction. He soon scampered away. Up easy-angled zig-zags on the rocky slopes, I soon reached the snow level and came across the first of the hordes of weekend ski-tourers descending after their early morning shifts.

Fortunately hundreds of ski tracks had compressed the snow enough for me not to have too much difficulty and I only sank in to my boot tops. By 10.15 a.m. I was at the delightful Refuge du Glacier Blanc and after a snack and a drink headed on up the glacier. Views soon opened up and I had a wonderful panorama of Barre des Ecrins, my goal, at the head of the wide valley. I continued on up. The last hundred metres were hard work up to the Refuge Ecrins – deep wet snow that I sank into – but by 12.30 p.m. I had arrived at 3294 metres, the highest I have been on this trip. Wonderful! Having met the hut guardian on his way down after the weekend, and having been informed that the hut was closed but the winter room was open, with no stove and water I was a little concerned about my liquid intake.

However, scouting round the back of the building, I discovered a huge vertical black scoop which normally would have had a pipe attached to it for taking off melting snow. So I collected a dixy and stuck it underneath and, lo and behold, within half an hour I had a good five or six litres of fresh water! Getting carried away with enthusiasm and the efficiency of the system, I managed to fill all the large pans in the hut and so provided a plentiful supply of water for all. By mid-afternoon I was joined by a keen young guided Italian party returning from their ski tour of that morning, and later on, a group of four Italians intent upon a ski tour of the Dom des Ecrins, then two German lads for the summit of the Barre.

Mountain huts are great – and all very different. In the height of the season (i.e. in a ski-touring area in the spring and in the main Alpine areas during July and August) they are usually teeming with people, and there's a guardian to see to the catering, which can run to three-course meals served with wine at the larger establishments. At these times they are noisy, hot and very sociable – but pretty unpleasant to sleep in. The dormitory-type accommodation becomes full to the brim – there is no chance of spare blankets, Europeans hate having the windows open for fear of draughts, and invariably the person in the next bunk snores. High season they are best avoided. The best time for huts is off-peak, even if this means parts of them are locked and what isn't will be cold, dark and uninviting.

The first thing is to get on a brew. It never ceases to amaze people how much liquid I can consume, both on and off the hill! On the hill I am convinced it helps towards better acclimatisation as the body adapts from living with plentiful oxygen at sea level to coping with less at higher altitudes. There is some evidence to back this up, but climbing is half psychological anyway and if I convince myself I'm adapting, then the chances are that I am!

Over the years I have experimented with various drinks for fluid replacement, and by a stroke of luck we had recently made contact with Wander UK who distribute an isotonic drink called Isostar. I had never tried it before, but was only too keen to give it a whirl. After a few weeks using it for fluid and mineral replacement following training runs in the UK, I was convinced that it would form part of my staple diet, keeping me fit and healthy during the physically taxing months to come. As we were donated a generous supply for the summer, I was able to use a plentiful amount to help maintain my body in tiptop condition.

The two older couples of Italians who arrived later that afternoon, steaming and happy to be there, were a mixed bunch. The men had years of adventure and experience behind them, you could see that from their kit, but their wives or girlfriends were much less experienced, with new skis, new kit and enjoying being out on a spree.

My Italian is non-existent and their English was nearly as bad, so whilst it would have been great to have some conversation we had to be content with waving our arms and smiling. The Barre Voie Normale was a big goal for them and they couldn't quite conceive my plan to do a climb and descend alone. I caught the older chap looking at me oddly from time to time.

JB: Alison's first night away on this trip. Would the children notice and will it bother them?

It was a lovely almost perfect spring day. Playing and exploring kept us busy. As the day drew on the children went to forage for wood. I broke it up and stacked it ready for the evening. They helped build and light the fire. I explained that I would sleep outside and in between their tents.

The night was the clearest so far. After bedtime stories Kate dropped straight into a deep sleep, tired out after hauling all that timber! Tom quietly chatted. We lay on our backs and star watched. After all the cloudy nights we had experienced, shooting stars were still a novelty.

The pine branches, dry as bone, crackled in the flames and lent a fragrant end to a wonderful, simple day. All we needed to make it complete was the weather to grant us two consecutive good days. That was all Alison needed to collect her first 4000-metre peak of the year. We had had one good day, could tomorrow be the same?

MONDAY 24TH MAY

Woken around 2.30 a.m. by the wind. At first I thought it was an animal on the roof, then realised it was the wind banging a shutter. Not a good sign. Back to dozing. 4.30 a.m. and the Italians' alarm went off. Up, ready to leave after cheese, crackers and Isostar around 5.20 a.m. Descended to the glacier and set off due west up the glacier following ski tracks until they branched right and north to climb steeply to the summit, Roche Faurio. I continued on to the base of the steeper section, past part-hidden ski tracks and knee-deep snow, ploughing uphill. Soon underneath the North Face I thrashed around in the blowing snow, trying to put on more warm clothes, changing gloves for warmer mitts, ski poles for axes, etc. Clouds are arriving, strong winds and continuous falls of spindrift.

I needed to hurry before it deteriorated too much. Now on steeper ground, I could climb more efficiently with my two Black Prophet tools and crampons, as I followed the narrow icy line of the Whymper Couloir on the North Face which led to the summit ridge. Visibility was low, but I knew when I had hit the ridge – I could go no higher, just turn right and head along to the summit. Deep wet heavy snow piled high on chaotic boulders, it was slow going. By 9.15 a.m. it started to slope down in all directions. This was the summit. No spectacular views, just wind-blasted snow in my face and grey cloud all around; time to go down. Continuing on down the narrow ridge, taking a bearing to check my direction, I followed the knife-edge ridge as far as a col, which I assumed to be the Brèche Lory – the gap between the snow cap of Dôme des Ecrins and the rocky summit of Barre des Ecrins. Here again I took a compass bearing for the change of direction; it was now a total white-out. No picking up ski tracks from yesterday's ski-tourers as I had hoped. I cautiously ploughed my way down through thick snow. Occasional breaks in the clouds helped me to locate the huge séracs and I tried to remember which way the ski tracks had wound their way up through them. Weaving left and then right, my progress was slow; I wanted to be cautious, there were some huge crevasses here. I contemplated digging into the snow and waiting until good weather arrived, but just then there was a clearing and I heard voices. I needed to go a long way to the right. I soon caught up with the two Germans who, in increasing bad weather, had turned back from my descent route, the Voie Classique, and in miserable conditions we descended to the glacier. The Germans skied back to the refuge for another attempt tomorrow. I walked down for brews and was forced to celebrate on wine with the two Italian couples who had had to retreat from their route after a late start from the hut.

It was time to head back to Chamonix. We had all enjoyed sampling the delights of Les Ecrins out of season and had cherished memories of wild camping, copious hot water, orchids by the score and Haldane Vegeburger-stealing marmots. Perkins did us proud. All I needed was for the weather to be as reliable. I replaced my stolen gear and waited. On 3rd June the long-range weather forecast was optimistic. I was fit; it was a chance to try and get one of the Big Six. I packed my rucksac and weighed up the options. With more fresh snow over the past few days I felt uneasy about the long glacier approach and descents of the Grandes Jorasses, so I plumped for my old favourite – the Matterhorn.

We packed up in glorious sunshine and Perkins picked up his thirty-odd years to trundle the family over the Col des Montets, down the smooth Swiss roads to the unlovely village of Täsch where JB and the children were going to camp.

JB: There is only just room for one campsite at Täsch, the car park with a village, squeezed between the railway and the steep valley side.

It was hot, humid and crowded. Alison, heavily laden, headed off to make the Hörnli Hut that night. I parked the children and their toys under a shady tree and got on with the camping.

The evening tourists and mountaineers returning to the campsite were apparently impressed to see a 'new modern man' alone with his children. Little did they know!

By 2.15 p.m. they had settled in at the site and I was off. I changed my clothes, shouldered my rucksac and jumped on the train up the valley to Zermatt. Things did not go well from the start. I rushed through the streets thronged with tourists to the end of the village only to discover that the Schwarzsee lift, my means of getting high, was shut until 25th June. Disappointed, I went outside to sit and study my map and weigh up whether time would allow me to walk up to the Hörnli Hut that night – only to discover another lift shown. I went back in and asked if I could get to the Furgg Station. Reluctantly the lady agreed and, assuring me that I had probably missed the last téléphérique, she still sold me a ticket and I dashed through the turnstiles. No one, nothing, and then ten minutes later a téléphérique arrived. Yes, I could ride up, but not back down. By 5.00 p.m. I was at the top station, by 5.30 p.m. I was at Schwarzsee and after knee-deep snow, at 7.30 p.m. I arrived at the Hörnli Hut.

Alone, I made myself comfortable in the kitchen with mattresses from upstairs and lots of blankets. With ample snow to melt down I was brewing until 10.30 p.m.

SATURDAY 5TH JUNE

Woke at 3.00, 3.30 and 4.00 a.m. It is hard to drop off again when you are keen not to oversleep. Finally up at 5.00 a.m., put the stove on to make a hot drink. Tried to force some breakfast down, but two Jordan's muesli bars were all I could manage. Inner boots, then outers on. I was startled by a noise outside; it turned out to be a guide who had come up for a training walk before his summer season started.

Soon I was ready to go. Sprayway Gore-Tex outers and harness on, I locked the hut shutters and set off. Only five minutes from the hut and I was sinking in the snow. Plodding up to my knees across the glacial system which spreads from the base of the North Face. Not a bad crossing of the bergschrund, the icefield was soft, but not in too bad a condition. I swing the Black Prophet tools, and away we go. As I got closer to the top of the icefield and the ramp I could see how unstable and unconsolidated it all was. Wet snow lay on top of smooth rock slabs. I crossed the rocky ridge towards the bottom of the next key section – the ramp – and contemplated. It looked wet, unstable and foolhardy.

Getting out my rope, I abseiled twenty-five metres off a peg back to the icefield and downclimbed now on wet and horrible snow. I was back with the family in Täsch by 3.00 p.m.

JB: Next morning we ambled downtown to the baker's, where four pounds sterling equivalent in Swiss francs bought us one family-sized loaf. It took me, a Yorkshireman, months to recover from that shock. The bouncy tourist office girl directed me to a fine playground next to the church. Tom came back from the vast sandpit with a cow, but it was only a plastic model.

The swings gave an excellent view of the station and campsite. Late afternoon, and a small heavily laden figure got off the train. It was time to go back down into the real world. A shoulder was obviously required.

Tired and disappointed, I began to feel negative about the whole trip. With the weather playing us hands like this, had I just bitten off more than I could chew?

We returned to Chamonix on a low. The mountains were just not playing ball. Back to our favourite campsite at Les Drus in the hamlet of Les Bois and I settled down once again to lots of long runs in the Aiguilles Rouges and days of rock climbing in the valley. My total meterage of rock climbing was high, but my score out of six was zero!

5

THE GRANDES JORASSES
– 4208m

The most formidable granite wall in the entire
Alps.

Alessandro Gogna

The Grandes Jorasses is a large mountain. However, since its mighty
North Face can only be seen from afar, it is not well known by sight to
the general public, unlike the Matterhorn, Eiger or Dru.

The French/Italian border traverses the crest of the North Face
which has six individual summits. Looking directly at the North Face
from the Aiguilles Rouges or Montenvers they are, from left to right,
the Pointe Walker (4208m), Pointe Whymper (4184m), Pointe Croz
(4101m), Pointe Hélène (4045m), Pointe Marguerite (4065m) and
Pointe Young (3996m). These names tell the story of the earliest
ascents. It is hardly possible to climb in the Alps without being aware
of all those who have gone before.

The first ascent of the mountain was made by Edward Whymper
with Michel Croz, Christian Almer and Franz Biener on 24th June,
1865. Three weeks later Whymper and Croz went on to the Matterhorn, but that is another story. The actual first ascent of the highest
Pointe was made by Horace Walker with Johann Juan, Julien Grange
and Melchior Anderegg on 30th June, 1868, three years later. The
other Pointes succumbed by the turn of the century. The summits had
now all been climbed by their easiest routes. Next came the minor
faces and ridges. The most appealing of these is the left-bounding east
ridge, the Hirondelles. This rises from the col of the same name and

The North Face of the Grandes Jorasses (4208m)

neatly frames the mountain's North Face. Geoffrey Winthrop Young's party descended the ridge in 1911 to examine the difficulties at first hand. They must have been impressed because they did not return. It was not climbed for the first time until 1927 and then by an Italian team whose successful ascent was doubted until the second ascent team discovered the pitons used by the Italians to climb the hardest section, the Fissure Rey, eight years later.

The North Face has two prominent spurs dropping down from the Pointes Walker and Croz. Splitting them at their base is a steep icefield with fingers of ice leading ever upwards. To the left of the Walker Spur lies an even steeper icefield and gully system. To the able climbers of this century the icefield separating the spurs must have looked the best line of weakness for future ascents and by the thirties all Alpine eyes were looking at the North Face and its unclimbed icefields and spurs. For the illustrious catalogue of those who tried them, see Appendix II.

The Croz Spur fell first, in 1935, and the second ascent team, a few days later, included the Swiss Loulou Boulaz, the first woman to climb the Spur. All eyes moved to the Walker Spur which succumbed to the Italians in 1938.

What next? Every climbing generation has its last great problem and the area of steep ice to the left of the Walker Spur was this for the sixties. It had been named by the French Le Linceul or the Shroud because of its shape and stonefall record! Robert Paragot, John Harlin and Dougal Haston all made various attempts. However, it was the evergreen and innovative René Desmaison and Robert Flematty who climbed it in the winter of 1968. Very bad weather and an exceptionally cold winter made their twelve days of ascent and descent something of a trial.

The last great problem for the seventies was the central icefield and its gullies which Chris Bonington's party failed on, and a Japanese team only succeeded by dint of laying total siege to the ice with loads of fixed rope. A way to the top maybe, but not one to emulate. It took the brilliant but famously scruffy British alpinist Alex MacIntyre to show the world that you did not need fixed ropes and expedition tactics which siege a route to death in order to succeed, just straightforward drive and talent. With Nick Colton, and starting late in the evening at the foot of the Walker Spur, he climbed through the night and into the next day to establish the hardest route yet.

After a mountain has been climbed by most of its main lines the next focus is usually solo and winter ascents of these. The Walker Spur was first climbed in winter in 1964 by Walter Bonatti and Cosimo Zappelli in storm conditions. René Desmaison with Robert Flematty had of course completed the first *and* winter ascent of the Shroud in 1968. It was again the innovative and maverick René Desmaison who laid siege to the massive rocky east flank of the Walker Spur in 1971 with Serge Gousseault. The winter was a hard one and the attempt ended when Serge Gousseault died in Desmaison's arms 150 metres below the top. Ten days of winter storms had exacted their price. Desmaison returned in 1973 along with Giorgio Bertone and Michel Claret to complete the climb.

Solo climbers were not far behind: Alessandro Gogna climbed the Walker Spur in 1968 and Jean Afanassief climbed the Croz Spur in 1972. Claims for the Shroud had some doubt until the winter of 1974 when it was definitely soloed by Ivano Ghirardini.

The Grandes Jorasses has always had a special appeal for me. I love its beauty and relative remoteness in comparison to many of the other great north faces.

We were camping at Les Drus, and at last the forecast was good. The météo promised two clear and sunny days. The previous day's fresh snow would, I hoped, freeze. Should I try something on the Aiguilles? I aired my enthusiasm for the Grandes Jorasses. In my initial plan of doing a solo climb on the North Face I had thought of either the Walker Spur or the Croz Spur. If conditions allowed, I should have loved to climb the Walker in rock boots and a chalk bag, but with its popularity these days I knew that it would be far too overcrowded. The majestic central spur of the Croz had always appealed too. What's more it was twenty-one years since its first solo, and it was still to be soloed by a woman.

As usual in these high mountains, conditions would dictate the safest and most sensible route of ascent. Only nineteen years previously the Grandes Jorasses had received its first solo via the Shroud, the icefield to the left of the Walker Spur; if conditions allowed, this would provide a suitable route for me, too. With no previous solo ascents by women it also proved a magnet. In recent summers it has remained very inconsistent due to the dryness of the seasons. If it were now to be continuous after all the late winter snow, that would be great. It was time to make my mark and I was raring to go.

JB fried up my main food, two pounds of Haldane cheese and onion vegetarian sausages, plus Isostar for drinks and Jordan's Frusli bars for fuel and dessert. I intended to be away for no more than two nights. At JB's suggestion I strapped my plastic mountain boots to the outside of my sac, donned my Reeboks and at 10.30 a.m., armed with adjustable ski poles for the long uphill trek, I left Les Bois for the North Face of the Grandes Jorasses and the Leschaux Hut.

JB: As Alison left I could not help wondering just how many top climbers would relish walking from the valley to the Leschaux Hut, doing a major route such as the Shroud, descending the Hirondelles Ridge and then walking all the way back down to the valley again. Pro climbing is certainly not glamorous and keeps you on your feet.

The children and I were off to the beach, well at least the granite sands and boulders besides the Arve. It would be clean, but it would be icy cold.

I headed into the woods and up the hill to Montenvers and a water bottle refill at 12 noon. At Montenvers I experienced a slight apprehension! Was the plan wise? Yes! I climbed down the ladders to the Mer de Glace and sat a moment, then tucking my Reeboks under a boulder for my return, changed into plastic boots and away on to the dirty ice, a jumble of cracks and slots. It took quite a while to reach the flatter central part in a steady plod, with occasional large steps over the cracks, then up the steeper central section before heading off left towards the Leschaux Glacier.

The temperature was kind. What can so often be a huge torrent to cross at the glacier centre in the midday sun proved only of mountain stream proportions. So with one leap I was over and heading for the higgledy-piggledy moraine of the glacial junction. Lots of ups and downs over the ice and loose boulders, working out the best route, and I headed to the true right bank of the Leschaux Glacier. On the Mer de Glace two guides descending from the Aiguille du Plan had asked my destination. They had had a hard enough time in waist-deep snow. 'Good luck,' was their response to my reply! Now on the Leschaux Glacier six more climbers came dashing down. Not even a word for the cat. I continued my solitary way upwards, making use of a big soft snow cone to get off the glacier on to the hut path. A marmot sat up to greet me, there were beautiful alpine flowers and a sparkling running stream, a good source of drinking water for later.

The Leschaux Hut was empty, and fairly tidy. The last entry in the hut book was from a Club Alpin Français (CAF) working/cleaning party. They had obviously not had the time to work on the kitchen! I took off my boots and socks, spreading them in the sun, unpacked my stove and got a drink on the go. Finding a suitable large water container, I slipped on some wonderful hut rubber galoshes and slid down the first snow slope to the path to fetch some water. It was early afternoon, plenty of time to sit and relax in the sun enjoying the magnificent views.

Later my prospect of peace was shattered as I saw four figures plodding slowly up the glacier beneath me. An hour later two young ambitious French guides arrived, then a pleasant French couple. I had looked forward to a quiet solitary evening to unwind, prepare myself and think – but in many ways it would be nicer with company. My stove was roaring and brews well on the go, which the guides were happy to share, if surprised by my presence. The French couple when they arrived were delighted to have made it to this remote hut, and expressed their glee by generously sharing chocolate and handing out cigarettes. For the guides and me it was just the starting point, the station at the beginning of the journey, but for them it was the adventure itself, and to share a hut with three real climbers at the end of it made their day complete.

My French was passable, but still limited. I found it very easy to make myself understood, but understanding the response was often far from easy. As usual, I think the guides assumed I was there just for a visit, though my gear hanging ready for the morning obviously roused their interest. But I was dismayed when I heard their plans were for the Shroud, too. I hadn't even contemplated anyone else heading for the same route. Only three climbers in the hut, all these hundreds of routes all round us, and we were bound for the same one.

It is very difficult to explain how you feel the night before a big climb or a major route, such as those I had chosen to do. Of course there is quite a lot of apprehension swilling about. As darkness creeps in, so do the doubts. Do I have the ability, do I have the self-confidence to carry it through? In European huts a lot of wine tends to get consumed by climbers acquiring the Dutch courage to answer these questions, but I've never had the spare cash to try this method of bolstering the morale.

Certainly the night before a climb is usually short, as climbers set off very early and the nervous ones toss and turn for most of the intervening hours. As solo climbing a route is essentially a speedy activity, there is generally not the need for me to be up with the first wave of departures, so the night is longer, but so is the waiting. I was hoping I would be able to complete the ascent and descent of the Shroud in one day and do the technical climbing in daylight, so I did not have to be stumbling around in the dark for an early start.

Before you go to bed you will have sorted through your gear, packing into the sac everything you are going to carry and leaving the clothes and items you will need to put on in a neat pile for the morning. In bed you go through the gear again in your head and you go through the approach route, double-checking everything. A forgotten crampon can't be returned for when you have reached the bottom of the climb and losing your way on the approach to the route could cost you the ascent. Every minor detail is equally important, adding up to the success of the climb.

But the waiting is the hardest bit. At least it is not as bad as all the waiting about involved in roped climbing, the hanging around on a belay stance waiting for your rope partner to join you or complete the pitch above. You have time to think about the cold, time to look at your watch and see the day racing by, time to reflect on the situation and the surroundings. With solo climbing you have none of that. You are on your own, in total concentration, from start to finish, your vision is tunnelled from the foot to the summit of your climb. You see the goal and carefully but swiftly you aim for it.

People have asked me if I think what I do is reckless. I would hope not. The hardest and most rewarding part is in getting it all right – following the correct approach, not getting lost on the route, descending the mountain safely into the valley and coming away with good memories but leaving no mark on the mountain. A fellow solo climber once told me that while completing a major route in the Alps one winter, he hadn't carried any spare gloves. When I asked why not his casual response was that there was no need and he had forgotten to pack them anyway. When I quizzed him about the fact he had not carried a map and compass to get off the mountain in the event of bad weather, he said he assumed he would meet someone else. It wouldn't be a problem. Maybe it was just male arrogance. Maybe I'm just soft. But to me both these omissions added up to recklessness.

Climbers greatly enjoy life. After all, they have many more climbs left to live for, so part of the satisfaction is minimising the risks, and as every good girl guide or boy scout knows, the trick is to be prepared.

Mountains can be big and grand, and when you're on your own they can be very daunting. Leaving the hut in the dark hours of the early morning can be a strange experience. But the mountains are there to be climbed and enjoyed not conquered. I feel when solo climbing more attuned to the elements than at any other time and without external influences to sway you, a sixth sense seems to come into play. If everything is right, you may be allowed to climb your mountain.

My immediate plans had been complicated by the appearance of the two French guides. I worried whether to let them go first and leave them long enough so that I would not need to overtake them, but take the risk of them knocking down ice and stones on to me. Or should I go earlier than I had planned and get out of their way? But that would mean approaching the climb through a fairly complicated glacier with fresh snow covering the crevasses *in the dark*. No, that was a silly idea which would be dangerous, if not too frightening – so I decided on the former plan. I looked at the luminous hands of my Rolex watch: 1.00 a.m. Rolex had given it to me, which was a warming reminder of other people's confidence in me. I relaxed and waited for the guides to get up and go, content in the fact I had made a decision. At 2.00 a.m. they were up and moving and by 2.30 a.m. they had gone. I sat up to turn on my stove and then laid back down for ten minutes' contemplation . . . The pleasant French couple had slept long enough and were excited at the prospect of climbing action. They came down to watch me leave.

It was 3.30 a.m. on Thursday, 17th June as I turned on my headlamp torch and descended into the dark night. Behind me the flash of a camera. They had taken my photograph. I picked my way along the path and traced my way back towards the snow cone, alone in my own little world of light. Poking the snow with my ski poles I was pleased and relieved to find the avalanche rubble had hardened considerably since the previous afternoon. Down to the glacier – I was on my way!

I headed slowly on up the glacier, periodically turning off my headlamp torch to look at the mountain's relief to make sure I was on course, and then back on with the torch to see where the holes were. As I plodded higher, the snow got deeper and my tracks were more pronounced. Falling into a crevasse was the last thing I wanted at that moment. Sinking in up to and past my knees made it hard work, but I was moving well. I was fired up and feeling strong. The young guides had been using short mountain skis and leaving good ski tracks, but they were not much use to me on foot.

Yesterday evening before night fell I had carefully noted a way to the base of the Shroud, but in the half light, as usual, things looked very different. I followed the line I had hoped was okay but as I got higher it led into an area of crevasses that could not be seen from below. I tried to the right. My ski poles went straight through indicating a hole under the snow. I tried to the left. Again my poles made holes appear underneath. I wondered about sitting and waiting for better daylight but decided to retrace my steps and try again. This time the glacier looked better and I could pick my way around the few small openings, right then left and straight up to the base of the Walker Spur. Soon safer and easier angled snow ice led up to the bergschrund that guarded the entry to the initial couloir of the Shroud. But easier angle meant deeper soft snow.

With the gradual drying out of the Alpine areas that has taken place in the last decade, glaciers are becoming more twisted and tortuous and what were straightforward approaches are now difficult, dangerous and time-consuming, particularly for solo Alpinists.

Crossing the bergschrund was no problem as the weeks of bad weather had helped to fill in the big gaps with snow. It just needed care and caution. It was time to place my ice tools, step off and up.

Seven o'clock in the morning was the hour to put the motor into top gear. The initial gully was steep, but the ice climbing was fun. Good névé soon ran out and gave way to thin ice laid on steep bald rock. I remembered the entry in the Leschaux Hut book by a poked-off New Zealander last summer: 'No ice on the Shroud – oh for an ice age!'

As each of the little ice runnels I was following ran out into rock, I would move left or right to another and remembering, as someone once advised me, that 'with long axes and hammers you can always reach past the hard bits' and so I continued through the thin section. I just wanted to keep on motoring.

As I reached the top of the steep section of the gully, the angle eased into the main icefield. I caught sight of the young French guides. Their much earlier start and ski approach meant that they were still some distance in front, traversing up and to my left. The most interesting technical ice climbing was over. The icefield became more monotonous and my speed reduced as I grew even more careful. I noticed the altitude now, and the fresh snow lying on old hard winter ice meant making hard kicks with the Scarface crampons for firm placements. Front two points just in the ice, heels resting on powder snow!

By now the Chamonix weather forecast had proved itself less than spot-on. 'Beau temps' indeed! Clouds had amazingly appeared from nowhere and I was in the middle of both the clouds and the icefield. Someone once described the Shroud icefield as '. . . like climbing on the outside of a cathedral roof, both underneath and above had disappeared.'

Following the natural line and slope of the icefield, I climbed on and up with my chin tucked in from the ferocious wind that had now sprung up and was blasting me with spindrift and icy particles. In the steep and narrow finishing gully that climbs up to the rocky flank of the Hirondelles Ridge I caught up with the two French guides. They were thrashing with the powder snow and were not at all happy in the strongly gusting wind and spindrift. Neither was I, for all the snow they were dislodging was being blasted down on to me! So it was easier to take cover until I had a 'French-free' gully above me. I burrowed deeply into my Sprayway Gore-Tex jacket and Malden fleece, waiting until they had climbed out.

Brushing yet more powder snow away from the rock, enjoying again the positive feel of the rock holds, I balanced upwards and soon reached the Hirondelles Ridge. It was 9.30 a.m. No views into Italy today. Just strong gusting wind, clouds and spindrift. But I was on top of the first of my Big Six and my months of training had paid off.

For the last six months I had been very gradually building this up with only short runs, but regularly. Most days I would start with a run before breakfast, sometimes two to three miles, sometimes longer, but always with some stretch of uphill. I found not only that it made me feel much more relaxed throughout the day, but it seemed to be a start to the mental preparation I was going to need. To go out in the wet and cold winter mornings required discipline; I always hated to leave the warmth of a cosy bed, but once out, things seemed better! After this very slow, gradual build-up of overall fitness, once in the Alps at the end of March I had stepped up my training. When we arrived in Chamonix I started not only on longer runs, but with much more uphill work, and much steeper. I no longer had the responsibility of the two children all day. JB was there to help with that, and I could concentrate on stepping things up to get in top shape. I found that long runs of two to three hours, with one thousand metres' ascent and a fair few miles, were too much every day, so quite often I'd do one once every two or three days and, with the valley rock climbing in between, this seemed to keep me fairly well tuned.

Our break in the Calanques had been good too. Whilst there was no altitude training, long uphill hikes, combined with lots of rock mileage, gave me a rock confidence and overall fitness confidence that I was happy with. Now I had finally been able to put this hard work to good use, making a safe, speedy ascent with fitness and confidence.

As soon as I stopped moving my temperature plunged, so I refuelled with a litre of Isostar (never known anything like it for rehydration!) and Jordan's Frusli bars. Then I climbed into all the spare clothing I had, changed my damp fleece gloves for warm fleece and Gore-Tex outer mitts and prepared to descend the ridge and back down the gullies into the Leschaux Glacier basin.

The French were crouched under a small rocky bulge, just up to my left. They had told me the night before that they intended to go up the summit ridge and down into Italy for a huge pasta supper. However, they sounded less and less enthusiastic as the wind gusted and the spindrift blew. Did I know the way down to France? I told them I could remember the key section – finding the top of the descent gully after descending to the Col des Hirondelles. A few minutes later they abandoned their pasta plan and decided to head down with me.

We pooled my 100 mm and their two 50 mm ropes for speed and set off abseiling and down-climbing. The top of the MacIntyre/Todd route was unbelievable. Above a rocky niche was a huge rock spire plastered in wind-driven snow forming beautiful and wonderful patterns and shapes.

Down the snow gully on the right, a climb up left to the ridge and a few more abseils down the steep rock walls (the crux pitches of the upward Hirondelles Ridge) found us perched on the edge of the Col des Hirondelles. We pulled the ropes and climbed down into the very centre of the col. Between the swirling clouds and bracing against gusts of strengthening wind and spindrift, we cast about until I found the top of the key descent gully system that leads down to the Leschaux Glacier. There was the telltale buttress and the entry slab, but where was the big shiny abseil bolt? No luck, today it was covered by several metres of ice and snow.

We down-climbed into the gully until we could find clear rock to set up the first of many abseils. A straight gully after the pinnacles of the ridge provided a very quick and efficient descent direct to the bergschrund. Just set up the ropes, all abseil down, pull the ropes and repeat . . . soon we were back on the Leschaux Glacier. As we moved down the ice we came out of the clouds and, relieved to be on more level ground, we chatted, ate our remaining food and degeared.

The next part of the descent looked a touch awkward. The freshly fallen snow was deep and had hidden most of the crevasses. Slight hollows and dips were going to be the telltale signs to watch out for. I set off. Right, left, right, sinking into the snow thigh deep. I ploughed on down. The two French with slight smiles donned their specialist mountain skis to begin their quick fun descent. Oh dear! They discovered that the snow was so sticky and fluffy that it balled up their skis and at every turn they fell over! Obviously a less enthusiastic and more cautious ski technique was required. Using my strong legs and ski poles I was able to keep up until the angle of the snow decreased. They could now glide on down without turning, but their legs were so tired that they just kept stopping for a rest and drinks. We chatted and then at a good pace we descended the easier section of the glacier together. The skiable snow was running out now so we had a long rest this time before the awkward descent down and through the twisted moraine of the Leschaux Glacier back to the Mer de Glace.

A long, long plod down the dirty ice to the Montenvers ladders. I peered under the boulder and with a grin produced my Reeboks. With absolute pleasure I took off my plastic boots and changed for the long flog back down into the valley, rewarding my feet for the descent. Desperate for a drink, I sped up the ladders to the Montenvers Station, but the only water was the run-off tank from the station roof. Everything was locked up. We passed a drinks vending machine but I had no money and the French after fumbling realised they did not have the correct change. Picking up the well-engineered track through the woods we headed down. Halfway down, I waited at the closed *buvette* to say my cheerios, but after ten minutes decided they must have headed towards Chamonix higher up.

I set off alone once more, so weary, every boulder was a tempting resting place. The fast-encroaching darkness and the forest of pine trees made it hard to see the path. Down, down, down. I thought I had lost the way, but realised in time that the dark made it seem so very different! Even the last two hundred metres along the flat lane to the camp site at Les Drus seemed a long, long way. It was 10.10 p.m. I dropped my rucksac by Perkins and unzipped the big tent. Kate was fast asleep. I peered in the other tent, Tom fast asleep. I so much wanted to hug and cuddle them. I slumped down on to the sledge, exhausted. I wanted JB, I knew I would cry!

A figure walked calmly and slowly out of the dark. He hugged me, pleased to see me whether I had climbed the face or not. It was me back safe that mattered. Bursting with pride I told him. A huge effort from so many had gone into the Big Six and after months of bad weather a great climb, on a great Alpine wall, in a fast time, was at last under my belt.

Too tired to move, I let JB spoil me. He poured litres of hot and cold Isostar down me to rehydrate me and then cooked up a huge pasta with mackerel sauce, topped off with grated cheese. How fantastic to be pampered. Fed and watered, sleep was rapidly overtaking me. I needed a hot shower, but it was too late, the showers had been turned off. JB poured bowls of hot water over me. Tiredness set in. My body started uncontrollably to tremble and shiver violently. What I needed was rest and sleep. Wrapped in yards of Malden fleece I snuggled into my bed, relaxed, and slept . . .

At the time it was difficult to evaluate my performance. I had walked from Les Bois (1083m) to the Leschaux Hut (2431m), climbed the Shroud (750m long), from 3010 metres to 3760 metres, descended the Hirondelles Ridge and Col, then walked all the way back to Les Bois. The simple ascent is 2677 metres, as is the descent; the distance as a round trip is around 33 kilometres. My ropeless solo of two and a quarter hours' climbing time, two and a half hours all told, may be the fastest on record and is the first solo by a woman!

JB: The time that a climber takes over a particular route tells a great deal about his/her performance. With the growth in interest by the media, particularly in Europe, unwritten but clearly understood rules have evolved for measuring this. Your climbing time is taken from when the technical climbing starts to its finish. This includes rests, but genuine hold-ups by other climbers etc. will be deducted from the total climbing time spent on the face.

Unless your ego needs constant massaging it is a good idea to round times up to the next quarter of an hour.

Alison's time on the Shroud sent shudders of disbelief around the Chamonix fleshpots. The fastest time ever, by a woman and not even French to boot! However, one of the Chamonix-based young guides whom she overtook was at least gallant and accurate in her praise: 'We set off ages before her, on skis, we are fit and good climbers. We looked down and she was on our heels . . .'

I took several days to recover and of course the weather was back to the awful normal for this year. I grabbed some valley rock mileage to keep in touch and, on a morning's good weather break, enjoyed a stolen mini Alpine classic rock solo on the South-south-east face of the Aiguille de la Glière in the Aiguilles Rouges.

Then we stocked up once more on supermarket food and cheap diesel and headed off to Switzerland on 24th June. Would we find a good weather slot and good conditions for No. 2 – the North Face of the Matterhorn? One down – five to go!

6

THE MATTERHORN –
4478m

> The most beautiful sight this region offers is the
> proud and lofty peak of the Matterhorn.
>
> Horace Bénédict de Saussure, 1789

The Matterhorn is surely the best recognised mountain in the world. Its perfect child-drawn shape has graced more calendars, book jackets, jigsaws, postcards, tea towels, videos, tee shirts, ashtrays and hats than any other. The Matterhorn is the only reason for the modern Zermatt, the sleek and expensive resort that lies at its Swiss foot.

On the border of Switzerland and Italy, the mountain has had a long and chequered history and the drama of the first ascent could have been scripted in Hollywood or lifted from the plot of a popular thriller.

The English, the French, the Italians were all active on the early attempts on what John Ruskin called 'the most noble cliff of Europe'. In 1862 the English reached and named Pic Tyndal, the Matterhorn's south-west subsidiary summit.

The main players however were Jean-Antoine Carrel and Edward Whymper, sometimes co-operating and sometimes in competition. By July 1865 Whymper had made eight separate attempts and for his proposed ninth found that Carrel could not come along since he had urgent business in the Aosta valley. In reality Jean-Antoine Carrel and his party were hotfooting it to Breuil on the Italian side of the Matterhorn to make their own attempt! Whymper was not fooled for long and he proceeded to Zermatt at all speed. What he found in

The Schmid route on the North Face of the Matterhorn (4478m)

Zermatt was more competition, but British this time. Charles Hudson with his young companion Douglas Hadow was intending to co-operate with Lord Francis Douglas who had secured the services of the leading Chamonix Guide Michel Croz. Croz had previously accompanied Whymper on many climbs and first ascents, amongst them being the Barre des Ecrins (4101m) and Pointe Whymper (4184m) on the Grandes Jorasses. Whymper joined up with this team and on 13th July, 1865, accompanied by Peter Taugwalder Senior and his son Peter Junior as porters from Zermatt, they set off to climb the Hörnli Ridge of the Matterhorn.

They bivouacked and Michel Croz with Peter Taugwalder Junior carried out an evening reconnaissance and came back with the great news that they had met with no particular difficulties.

The party started climbing as soon as it was light on 14th July which eventually turned out to be one of those oh so perfect climbing days with amazingly clear visibility. They climbed mainly as roped pairs until they reached the shoulder. Here the roped order was Croz, Whymper, Hudson, Hadow, Douglas with the two Taugwalders last.

They found the rock on the shoulder snow-covered in parts with some verglas from previous storms. Croz led and traversed off the ridge crest on to the North Face which led to tricky climbing up vertical rock to regain the ridge. They were then greeted by a short easy snow slope which ran up to the summit ridge.

Croz and Whymper untied from their companions and made a quick dash to the summit, which according to Whymper ended in a dead heat at 1.40 p.m. The Matterhorn had been climbed for the very first time, or had it?

The summit ridge has two high points, one at each end. One is in Switzerland and one in Italy, the side from which Carrel was climbing. Which was the highest and had Carrel and his team beaten them into second place? Whymper, impatient, shot along the ridge towards Italy. At the far end he peered down. Joy of joys, he could just make out, way below, Carrel and his team. He summoned Croz across, they shouted news of their success down to Carrel, and when the Italians did not respond Whymper levered rocks from the summit ridge and rolled them down upon his rival. Carrel and his team beat a hasty retreat, no doubt less than pleased with being beaten to the first ascent and with Whymper's calling cards!

Back at the Swiss and highest summit they built a cairn and Croz placed a tent pole with his shirt on it to mark their victory. This was seen in Zermatt and also in Breuil where they patriotically but wrongly assumed that Carrel had triumphed. Then after Whymper and his team built a second cairn on the Italian summit, just to rub it in, they took in the exceptional panorama which from Whymper's own account must have been amazing. They were clearly able to see the Finsteraarhorn in the Bernese Oberland, the Disgrazia, the Ortler, Mount Viso (about 100 miles or 160 kilometres away as the crow flies), the Alpes Maritimes, Les Ecrins, the Graians and, lastly, shining in the perfect light, the highest peak of western Europe, Mont Blanc – what a sight it must have been!

They remained on the summit ridge for over an hour. It was time to return. Whymper and Hudson discussed the proposed descent and the roped order. They started down as separate roped pairs, but Lord Francis Douglas requested that they re-form as a single rope of seven. This they did and the order of descent was Croz, Hadow, Hudson, Douglas, Taugwalder Senior, Whymper and Taugwalder Junior last.

All went well until, at a tricky rock wall where Michel Croz was helping the less experienced Hadow to place his feet, Hadow slipped, knocking Croz from his footholds. Their combined weight coming on to the rope dragged Hudson from his steps and he in turn pulled down Douglas. The falling weight of the first four came jointly on the Taugwalders and Whymper. The three held their ground, but the rope snapped below Taugwalder Senior and with horror they saw their companions sliding and accelerating down into the North Face and to their certain death. Whymper wrote, 'So perished our comrades.'

Stunned by what they had seen, the three survivors remained rooted for at least thirty minutes. Whymper began to organise their descent but at first neither of the Taugwalders would budge. However with some encouragement young Peter climbed down to join his father and Whymper. They stood together, Whymper coiled up the remains of the snapped rope (which still exists today and for a price can be viewed in the Zermatt museum) and they started their nervous descent. Just to add to their discomfort a huge colourless arc formed in the sky above Mount Liskamm. This further unnerved the Taugwalders who took it as a sign of displeasure from the gods. They slowly climbed down and it must have been a sorely tired and harassed team that were forced by nightfall into sleeping out on the ridge. 'After six miserable hours on a wretched slab', wrote Whymper, they continued down next morning into Zermatt.

The following day Whymper, accompanied by other British climbers and their guides, climbed back up to recover his companions. Croz, Hadow and Hudson were found in the order of their fall. Their graves and memorials are in Zermatt churchyard. The body of Lord Francis Douglas was never found

The accident created a furore in the press of the day. More fuel was added to the controversy at the Valais Government enquiry, when Peter Taugwalder Senior gave a differing account of the accident to that of Whymper, then under repeated cross-examination changed his mind and his story. For many years there was rumour and suspicion locally that Taugwalder Senior had cut the rope between himself and the lower four. The reputation and the lure of the Matterhorn was born that day and continues to this.

Climbing, like life, does not stand still and Carrel and his team returned a few days later to climb the Italian ridge. Ambitious climbers then looked at the remaining two ridges, and in 1879 the great A.F. Mummery, Alexander Burgener, Johann Petrus and Augustin Gentinetta climbed the Zmutt Ridge, and the Furggen Ridge finally fell to Mario Piacenza, Jean-Joseph Carrel and Giuseppe Gaspard in 1911. The next few years saw a gradual filling-in of the blanks, but by the end of the 1920s the ever ambitious German-speaking climbing world was looking towards the great Alpine north faces.

Gaston Rébuffat described the North Face in his book *Men and the Matterhorn* as:

Of the four faces of the Matterhorn the North Face is the most severe, the most beautiful and the most awe-inspiring; it is between the Hörnli arête and the Zmutt arête and is 3500 feet in height. Seen from the front, from Zinalrothorn, it has the simplicity of a perfect triangle. Seen from Zermatt it has the appearance of a gigantic twisted coil of stone. To look at it seems difficult, but first and foremost it is dangerous. The rock is bad, the ice on it glassy, there are no halting places or the slightest protection in case of storm, but above all there are avalanches of rock . . . The Matterhorn is strange and always mysterious. Many dreamed of it yet few dared to try.

Of course climbers came. In 1923 the Austrians Franz Piekielko and Alfred Horeschowsky (the originator of all modern ice hammers) attempted the North Face from the Hörnli Ridge. Two Swiss guides,

Kaspar Mooser and Victor Imboden, attempted the face in 1928, but at the righthand side. Mooser returned in 1930 to try the lefthand icefield, but was soon turned back by heavy icing.

In July 1931 two German brothers from Munich cycled to Zermatt. They were Franz and Toni Schmid. They started their attempt before dawn on 31st July by the lefthand icefield. They obviously had cold conditions as Toni Schmid wrote, 'Metre by metre we advanced . . . our fingers, scraped raw, were bleeding . . . we had to get away from that fearful ice wall. The ropes, stiff with frost became difficult to handle . . . With ever greater difficulty I still pressed on . . .' They bivouacked, hanging from two pitons, for a long cold night. Toni took the lead on the second morning but icy rock stopped his progress. Franz tried and even suggested that they retreated, but after some brisk dialogue he pressed on and gradually they made ground. The weather got worse and each urged the other to climb with greater speed. The storm broke just below the summit and was in full flow when at last they topped out. 'What did the unfettered elements matter . . . We ran along the arête [the summit ridge] to hide our ice axes near the iron cross [Italian summit] and a few metres lower down we found shelter under an overhang at the moment the storm reached its climax. There beneath the protection of our bivouac sheet, our hands met in a silent grasp.' The storm did relent and allowed them to start their descent of the Hörnli Ridge. A second storm caught them on the Shoulder and they fought their way down to the Solvay emergency shelter hut. All the next day they slept until the storm lashed itself out and on 3rd August they descended to a triumphal welcome in Zermatt. The first of the great Alpine North faces to be climbed, and by rank outsiders! There are always ambitious and talented climbers, whose achievements show the way forward.

On 22nd July, 1959, Dieter Marchardt, without fuss or show, completed the first solo ascent. Sadly, he soon perished trying to be the first climber to solo the North Wall of the Eiger.

Equipment and clothing improved and winter ascents became a more comfortable proposition. The media was interested and suddenly a north wall in winter was the place to be seen. There were three separate attempts in 1961. 1962 saw more teams in action. The first were Toni Kinshofer, Toni Hiebeler (part of the first team to climb the Eiger North Wall in winter), Erik Krempke and Pierre Mazeaud (French MP and no lover of English competition: 'It is not me they insult but the whole of France!'). They were highly organised and climbed well, but eventually they were forced off the face on to the Hörnli Ridge by bad weather. At the end of January the lesser-known trio of Adolf and Franz Huber and Hubert Sedlmayer made a bold attempt but again the winter weather played its hand and they were forced to escape to the Hörnli Ridge yet again.

Hilti Von Allmen and Paul Etter, who had tried in 1961, returned and fixed ropes on the face, then on 3rd February set off on their summit bid. They were closely followed by the Austrians Leo Schlommer and Erik Krempke, who were in turn closely followed by the German team of Werner Bittner, Peter Siegert and Rainer Kauschke. For the record Hilti Von Allmen and Paul Etter reached the summit first and newspapers and TV kept the public on the edge of their seats.

The *direttissima* cult that was to prove such a powerful draw on the other faces for modern climbers was a complete flop here as there is only one natural or apparent line – the Schmid route. So what firsts were left for this North Face? The first woman's ascent went to Yvette Vaucher who climbed the Schmid route in 1963 accompanied by her husband Michel Vaucher and Michel Darbellay (first solo ascent of the North Wall of the Eiger and first winter ascent of the North Face of the Piz Badile). During February 1965 Walter Bonatti tried to complete the Mooser/Imboden line, starting at the righthand side of the North Face, accompanied by Gigi Panei and Alberto Tassotti. They spent four days on the face, but Bonatti's abysmal luck with the weather eventually drove them down.

Bonatti stayed on in Zermatt and on 19th February he went back to the North Face, back to the line he had tried before. This time he succeeded and reached the summit on 23rd February, his last major climb before retiring to adventure journalism. It was the first winter solo ascent and the second route on the face. The Czechs and Japanese have added new starts to the original route, but they are really meaningless, as no two teams can follow the same line up this continually shifting face of loose rock and ephemeral ice.

However, the North Face had not yet been soloed by a woman.

Like many other people, I fell in love on first sight with the Matterhorn, ten years ago. Its perfect mountain shape appealed to my adventurous nature and, as my attempts to climb it have never been straightforward, it has retained its special allure. My first (and roped) attempts on its great North Face with Ian Parsons took us three visits finally to get to the summit.

Conditions on mixed faces have changed a lot, particularly over the last few years and I had no idea in what state I would find the face this time. The weather could be kind and the conditions superb – or things could be bad and the face dry. I'd just have to wait and see.

We decided to go up to Zermatt and stay there until the face was in condition. Our resources would not run to continued fleeting visits in and out of the valley, not at two Swiss francs to the pound sterling. So packing up as many provisions as we could, we parked Perkins at Visp Station and, with the excited children, moved up to the tiny campsite in Zermatt by train.

This time I did not have to hang about. We settled in at midday and I was off up Zermatt main street at 3 p.m.

JB: The campsite at Zermatt is basic but only a couple of minutes from town. Tom, Kate and I went into town so that Alison could slip away unnoticed. Kate really did not like to see her mum leave, but did not mind her being away.

The town was crowded with tourists of every shape, size and nationality. The children's playground is nicely tucked in beside the tennis courts and temporary Post Office. The playground was dominated by the children of the guest workers, who used to be Portuguese, but they have been undercut by the Yugoslavs. Three grim mothers held the central bench, knitting and scowling at all the incomers. They reminded me of the three witches of Macbeth, *only not so attractive. Their children were charmless and particularly hard on the Swiss young-sters. I wondered why! Tom and Kate got on fine, until the game of sand-throwing into small girls' eyes to make them cry. Tom, upset, asks what to do. I tell him to retaliate, but not with sand. The best right hook I have ever seen and the leading bully is howling as best he can with his bloody nose. His mother is not amused and she and the witches pounce on Tom. I intervene and it requires all my Yorkshire charm to stop them assaulting him. Who says that solo climbing has all the excitement. It did nothing for my popularity amongst the guest workers, but it brought a great deal of pleasure to the rest of the parents.*

Zermatt has one of the great toy shops. Hours were spent admiring what we could not afford. The sales assistants were generous to two well-behaved English children and plied them with leaflets, much to their delight.

I arrived at the Hörnli Hut two and a half hours later. Company this time consisted of a grumbling German who was looking for a partner for the Hörnli Ridge, and was not specially pleased when an unlikely partner like me came through the window. All evening he went on and on about helicopters, a death wish (his), and how a storm would arrive next day! But morale lifted as I saw three climbers, way down below, heading slowly up. More climbers must mean the weather forecast could not be too bad, or could it? When they arrived they informed me they did not know anything about the weather. They were two British brothers and the girlfriend of one of them. Their trip had been planned months ago, they'd come anyway.

I woke at 2.00 a.m., and went downstairs to weigh up the weather and prepare. No rush, I didn't really want to start climbing before dawn, but it was too late to return to bed. At 3.30 a.m. I headed out. It was cold and very windy. This concerned me. I assumed that a fast and strong wind would bring in different weather. I watched the clouds race by and headed down to the North Face and the icefield.

Snow was blowing around in the strong wind, as were small stones. Should I go on? I did not like the idea of another failure. On the other hand being wind-blasted by snow and stones, together with cloud and storms on the summit and descent, did not appeal. Three times I soloed up and down the bottom few pitches of the icefield. I stopped and looked at the rapidly changing cloud shapes. I hesitated, and then started to descend; I really wanted to go on, but something inside me told me to go down.

Back at the hut, I ungeared, had a drink and went back to bed. It was still early. It would be a long day. I decided to wait until next morning. The nervous German seemed startled. 'What has happened?' he asked.

We had breakfast, many brews and chatted. The wind got stronger and stronger. The grumpy German was unhappy and said he was going down. Good! The British trio decided to stay put, keen to do the ascent of the Hörnli. The clouds blowing off the Matterhorn were wild, swirling and wonderful. Ice crystals were forming, it was so cold. Here we were in June, and I was fully clad in silk, fleece underwear, fleece salopettes and thick fleece jacket, even in the sun! The British team and I pooled food for a fine evening meal, and drank their celebratory bottle of champagne to save carrying it back down! The clouds had come right down. But there was plenty of wood to burn for copious brews and a warm hut. We watched the clouds and whirl-winds of snow . . .

I woke at 3.30 a.m. Horror! What if the weather was going to be good after all and I wasn't ready to use it? I looked out of the hut and saw stars, a clear sky and no clouds. Slipping on boots, I stepped outside. A gust of wind greeted me as I walked around the hut and discovered the top of the Matterhorn was missing, lost in the clouds. Back inside. Half an hour later the cloud came rapidly down further and the wind increased. The Matterhorn did not want me to climb today! I returned to bed for a while and watched through the window as the tiny wind clouds on the tops of all the 4000-metre peaks around gradually grew into a cloudy and grey morning. I packed up and said goodbye to the British trio who were staying on until after lunch. They insisted I borrow a Black Diamond ice hammer, as mine had been stolen, which was very kind and trusting. (I was able to return it to them personally at a mountaineering trade show in September.) Back in Zermatt I felt disappointed but would be able to establish the weather pattern and start again.

Zermatt has long abandoned anything but a commercial interest in the climber and his world. I would call in at the guides office on the main street to ask about conditions on the mountain and the weather forecast, only to receive a bland face politely but firmly pointing me back down the street to two computerised weather stations in competing banks.

However, all is not lost, as long as Frau Paula Biner, the Grande Dame of Swiss mountaineering, is alive and kicking and holding court at the real climbers' home, Hotel Bahnhof. Whether an Alpine novice on your first visit, an ennobled lord or a world-class climber, the careful warm greeting is just the same. Her help and advice over the years has been greatly sought and appreciated, continuing the long tradition of her sadly missed brother, Bernard.

I called in at the Bahnhof to see Frau Biner and, helpful as ever, she rang around for me to see what was happening. By mid-morning I was back at the campsite, and there was a note from JB saying they were all at the park. He smiled at me as I came round the corner. He knew instantly that I had not done it but that did not matter. Tom came running across for a cuddle. Kate stayed on the swings, unconcerned. JB wanted to talk, Tom wanted attention and I needed consolation and reassurance. Later we walked through Zermatt as the children showed me all the wonderful toyshop windows.

Should I go straight back up the same day? JB thought that I ought to rest and go up again tomorrow. Although I feared I might miss a good weather slot, I felt I owed it to Tom and Kate to stay the night with them. Once I had missed the last téléphérique, I felt a lot happier.

Tom, Kate and I had a wonderful time in the park next morning. They both had hours of me pushing the swings. We returned to the campsite for lunch where JB had cooked an enormous pasta to feed us all (they would have bread and jam for tea) and stoke me up for tomorrow! Then JB went off with the children to the park and half an hour later I was packed, changed and ready to go. By 3.45 p.m. I was at the Hörnli Hut again.

There were three Scottish doctors still on the Hörnli Ridge from that morning and three Slovaks outside the hut on the terrace, with whom I shared copious bowls of tea.

TUESDAY 29TH JUNE

Woke about 3.15 a.m. Gator neoprene socks over my Polisox polypro inners, inner boots on. Folded my blankets and went downstairs to put the stove on. Slipped on my plastic outer shells and climbed out of the window to look at the weather and go to the loo.

It was not cold, but clear as a bell and with very little wind. 'Great!' Back in for Isostar and hardboiled eggs. Then leaving the Hörnli Ridge-bound Slovaks to their breakfast, I geared up and set off into the night. It was just after 4.00 a.m. It was starting to get light and my headlamp torch was not essential all the time. I knew exactly where to go and headed up the ridge and then across and down to the start of the climb.

There was some soft snow to get to the bergschrund, which I cautiously passed on hands and knees to spread my weight.

By just after 5.00 a.m. I was climbing. On my previous attempts I had been able to romp up and down the icefield without difficulty, but now the snow had compressed a little making the top layer somewhat thinner, so a little more awkward to get good foot placements on the old ice underneath. Cautiously I moved up. The higher I climbed, the more I could see the dawn rising behind me over the lofty tops of the Dom, Täschhorn and the Alphubel.

I smiled at my position and revelled in the thought that finally I was on my way. As I rose towards the top of the great icefield I weighed up the route I would take from there. I needed to get into a right-sloping ramp that would lead steeply on up through the middle section of the mountain. But getting there would be the key.

I recalled my ascent with Ian Parsons in 1984, when after a deep breath I had gone for it, off the ice and up on to a steep corner, only to be greatly relieved to find a peg in place to which I could belay and bring Ian up to me.

Now conditions were very different. With dry summers, the icefield had shrunk back, leaving a much longer area of thin mixed ground to cross before one could get into the ramp. I weighed up the possibility of going down right a little, then up. Whilst a lot steeper, the rock looked very solid and positive. But, on the thin icy patches on the rock I was on, I did not fancy the descending traverse. So instead I plumped for straight up.

There were some tricky moves reaching from one icy patch laid on the rock to another, then I was established in the ramp. It was no time to relax. From there the climbing looked hard and insecure. A very thin veneer of ice was laid on top of the rocky slabs and I picked my way up, precise and gentle with each tool placement. To hit too hard would only break up the ice around the picks and render them useless. Whilst getting secure pick placements was difficult enough, getting secure footholds was even harder. The front points of my crampons bit through the ice, only to grate and scrape around on the rock beneath. I was glad I was a delicate climber and not two stones heavier!

This insecure climbing made very nerve-racking and tiring work. I continued weaving right and left, following the natural line of the ramp, kept going by the thought that as soon as I reached the top of the ramp, I would be two-thirds of the way up the face. The angle of the wall would ease from there, so theoretically I should find things easier and so be able to increase my slow pace.

But it was not to be so. As I finally headed out of the ramp line and ice runnels, I came into very dry rocky ground plastered throughout with a layer of powder snow. All the rock holds had to be cleared before I could use them and everything felt very insecure. My hopes of easy motoring up the face in record time, in perfect snow conditions, were shattered. It became a time-consuming laborious task.

The cloud was closing in and the wind picking up. As I saw the

Zmutt Ridge come creeping in from the right, the higher I climbed, the nearer I knew I must be to the top. As the North Face draws to an end, the Zmutt and Hörnli Ridges close in on it from the right and the left respectively. I could see the Hörnli Ridge close by on the left and relief started to creep in.

The tiny haven of the Solvay emergency shelter was now well below. Remembering to move across rightwards to pick up the final gully system, soon I was there, the summit cross in front of me. I felt moved to tears. I had finally soloed the North Face of the Matterhorn.

For some reason I felt a special relationship with this mountain. The Matterhorn had finally let me climb its North Face, but it was not rewarding me with a view. The length of the border ridge was as far as I could see.

It was nearly 10.30 a.m., cloudy and rapidly warming up, no time to revel in my lofty position. Far into Italy I could discern the occasional flashes of lightning and hear the wild rumble of thunder creeping towards me. I needed to go down as fast as I could, and remembered from my past two experiences what a long and time-consuming descent it could be.

I set myself into steady continuous gear. The first steep section of rock was soon under my belt. I moved smartly across the flat section of the ridge and, pausing a moment to remember the catastrophe of the first ascent, headed rightwards, off the shoulder and down on to warm wet slopes of snow. Occasionally using for abseil points the great metal stakes driven deep into the rock to ease the guided climbs, I was making progress. As the lightning flashed around me and spots of rain turned into heavier bursts, I smiled at the fact that yet again I was not to take things for granted.

Heading on down and slightly right of the ridge crest, I decided to try a more direct line on the very edge. However, as I got to the crest, I felt an amazing tingling sensation and realised that my hair was standing on end – not a good place to be. So I darted quickly back to the more sheltered line I had previously followed. I could now see the tiny Hörnli Hut way down below.

I was tired mentally and physically and the realisation that I would not make it all the way to the valley that night, only to the hut, gave less urgency to the situation, and although the storm was raging around me, I felt calm.

Seventeen hundred metres later and 6.00 p.m. found me on the flat of the ridge and traversing towards the hut. Having assumed that I would be alone in the hut, it was with absolute pleasure that I smelt a whiff of woodsmoke from the chimney.

Uplifted, I raced round the hut and climbed in through the window. My three friendly Slovaks, Peter, Lator and Marian, were in residence, back after one of them felt ill attempting the Hörnli Ridge earlier in the day, and there was a young Swiss lad, anxious to find out the conditions on the mountain. They gave me a celebratory drink and lots of brews through a marvellously unwinding evening.

I was on the first téléphérique down to Winkermatten next morning, waiting patiently outside for the Zermatt Co-op to open to buy shampoo. At the baker's I picked up three almond croissants for our treat – I did not have enough cash for four. Then I called in at the Hotel Bahnhof to leave some mittens I had recovered on my descent, which I assumed belonged to the Scottish doctors. Frau Biner seemed both surprised and delighted that in such weather I had become the first woman to solo the North Face and in under five and a half hours. She said she was so pleased for the British and asked if I would return later with the family to write in Bernard Biner's book.

JB: A lie-in this morning, and a complete read through the story books. Then a smiling face with tears pushes through the tent entrance. At last number two is in the bag. On with the MSR for brews and the simple pleasure of Alison, Tom and Kate scoffing their celebratory croissants.

Yop and Roy, the Dutch anthropologists, buy Alison some wine and I make a huge pasta meal that spreads out into an afternoon feast. We may be poor and the exchange rate lousy, but we do know how to celebrate and enjoy ourselves.

After lunch we returned to Frau Biner. My hand was nervous with sweat after reading through Bernard Biner's book and finding the names of all my childhood heroes. I had to use my handkerchief to stop smudges as I entered my own ascent. Sitting with Paula for tea afterwards, it was a pleasure to see her pride as she reminisced about the great days of Bernard, while we discussed the earlier entries.

·I now needed a couple of days to unwind and rejuvenate, with a playground and a paddling pool for Tom and Kate and a swimming pool for me to exercise in gently. The Visp campsite was ideal for this, while I considered what to try next.

Logistically it had to be the Eiger.

A new variation on the
Lauper Face of the
Eiger (3970m)

MITTELLEGI RIDGE

HÖHENEIS

7

THE EIGER – 3970m

*Compared to the first ascents of the North Faces of
the Matterhorn and Grandes Jorasses, the Eigerwand
may be said to possess little or no mountaineering
value. The true route up the Eiger's North Face was
discovered in 1932.*

Alpine Journal, 1938

The Eiger and its northern faces has had more column inches lavished
on it than any other mountain in the world. A railway runs beneath its
famous faces up to a station and junction at Kleine Scheidegg. Here
one line continues down to Wengen and the other goes uphill to a
small station, Eigergletscher, where they keep huskies, and then
through long tunnels passing right through the mountain to arrive
at the highest station in Europe, the Jungfraujoch. The railway was
begun in 1912 and was the most expensive to build in the world at that
time. Eiger-watching could not be easier; there are even fixed coin-
operated telescopes at Kleine Scheidegg to allow tourists to watch the
climbers on the notorious Eigerwand.

The lefthand side of the North Face is cut off from the bulk of the face by
a series of pillars. When looked at from the valley, a natural climbing line
can be pieced together. Hans Lauper and Alfred Zurcher with A. Graven
and J. Knubel climbed this on 20th August, 1932. But the Nordwand or
wider righthand side of the face was quite another matter. So much drama
and controversy have surrounded this wall, so many classic books have
been written about it that I will only touch on the highlights.

The first real attempt to get any distance up the face was made by
the Germans Max Sedlmayer and Karl Mehringer in August 1935.

They started in the middle of the Eigerwand and climbed straight up. Dougal Haston, who attempted this section of the route with far better equipment in 1966, was 'struck by its difficulty'. Sedlmayer and Mehringer finally ground to a halt at what became known as the Death Bivouac, above the Third Icefield. A storm came in and they started to retreat. What actually happened next varies with the account you read. All that is certain is that they became the first victims of the Nordwand (North Wall) or, as the German newspapers later dubbed it, the Mordwand (Murder Wall).

The Swiss authorities grew twitchy and went so far as to pass a law forbidding climbers to attempt their wall. Sense dawned when they realised it was unenforceable and it was repealed. There was also an understandable Swiss nervousness about so many of the climbers being German and Austrian with possible Nazi backing. More of this later.

1937 brought the first of the well-publicised dramas that made Eiger-watching a ghoul's delight. Two Austrians, Edi Rainer and Willy Angerer, teamed up with two Germans, Andreas Hinterstoisser and Toni Kurz. They followed a start Rainer and Angerer had pioneered earlier as far as the Rote Fluh, and then Hinterstoisser led them across a traverse to open the way to the icefields. They climbed the First, Second and Third and their highest point was just below the Death Bivouac. Willy Angerer had been injured and it looked to watchers below as if the team had all decided to come down, which they did with speed and efficiency as far as the top of the First Icefield. As was to be expected, the weather broke and a storm lashed the face. Next morning they continued down to the end of Hinterstoisser's traverse. But this time neither Hinterstoisser nor Kurz could climb it in reverse. In the end they decided to try to abseil and climb straight down. This ended in disaster. Hinterstoisser fell to his death; Angerer was strangled by the rope and Rainer, also still attached, had frozen to death. Only Toni Kurz was left alive. The local Swiss guides attempted to rescue him from the railway tunnel which led on to the face. Kurz managed to descend until they could see him, but because of the overhanging nature of this stretch of the wall, they were just unable to reach him. He died hanging on his abseil ropes.

However, this brave attempt showed the way for others, even if Edward Strutt, the reactionary editor of the *Alpine Journal* derided all attempts as 'an obsession for the mentally deranged'. Further attempts in 1937 took the route up to the Ramp and added one more fatality to the death toll.

1938 began with two more deaths, but there were still many climbers of all abilities hanging around Alpiglen, Grindelwald and Kleine Scheidegg. Rumours abounded that the Germans and Austrians were sponsored by the Nazis. The world watched. It was the year the British Prime Minister Chamberlain would take a plane to Munich and return with a piece of paper.

Now the Austrians Heinrich Harrer and Fritz Kasparek were on the face. They were followed by two more Austrians, Rudi Fraissl and Leo Brankowsky. There was a surprise waiting for them, because already above them were Germans, Anderl Heckmair and Ludwig Vörg. The meeting must have been interesting to say the least. 'The six of us stood and laughed a little forcedly at the coincidence,' wrote Anderl Heckmair.

All six bivouacked and in the morning the weather unsettled. Heckmair and Vörg had already decided that the weather was going to break and they went down, all the way to Alpiglen where they checked the forecast, discovered they were wrong, and resolved to return to the face next day.

They must have climbed like steam, because by 11.00 a.m. they were at the upper reaches of the Second Icefield. At 11.30 they caught up with Harrer and Kasparek. (Fraissl had been hit by a stone fall the previous day and he and Brankowsky had climbed down in good order.)

As Heckmair recalls, 'It was a tricky situation. We were faced with the grave decision whether to overtake and press on, leaving them to their fate. I was close to doing this, but not Vörg, who was far better natured. It was he who found the redeeming words: 'Then let's form one party and rope together.''' So began one of the most dramatic chance combinations in climbing history.

They continued to climb as two separated ropes and soon Heckmair and Vörg, who led, passed the previous high point, which Vörg had reached the year before with Matthias Rebitsch. Up the Ramp they climbed and at 7.00 p.m. decided to bivouac. Heckmair scoffed a tin of sardines and paid the price during the night. Next morning they carried on up the Ramp, with Heckmair in the lead. Some hard climbing had them joined in one rope of four, but as they started the long traverse right, which became known as the Traverse of the Gods, they climbed as two separate ropes again, eager to reach the Spider and discover the route ahead. But the Eiger was not going to let them off lightly and an impressive storm set in. The Spider, a steep icefield at the base of the gullies leading to the summit ice, was no place to be.

Rain, sleet, snow, thunder and lightning must have made for exciting climbing. They kept going. An avalanche struck Heckmair who had the presence of mind to stab his pick into the ice. 'I held on to the pick with one hand and with the other grabbed Wiggerl [Vörg] by the scruff of the neck, convinced that our comrades had been swept away.'

They nearly had been, but with some hard climbing, rope manoeuvres and luck they were all united on one rope. They pressed on, and the weather improved slightly. They bivouacked again, this time on rock and ice. It was uncomfortable and insecure. During the night avalanches continued to slide over them. The snow persisted. They climbed on up the Exit Cracks. The going was hard, the rock ice plastered. An overhang caused problems and Heckmair was pulling out all the stops.

'The point of the ice piton on which I was clinging for dear life only went in a little way and so did the pick of my ice axe . . .

'Suddenly the piton came out, and at the same moment my axe gave way . . . Then I came off . . .

'Just as I fell I turned outwards. Wiggerl let the rope drop and caught me with his hands, and one of the points of my crampons went through his palm.'

Heckmair climbed back up and this time kept going, upwards. Nothing could stop them now and although the summit icefield was steep and exciting they made it to the top. Here they very nearly walked over and fell down the south side. Tiredness and bad visibility playing equal parts, the descent of the South-West Ridge and Flank was a living nightmare. The storm still raged, but at last they dropped out of bad weather and wondered if they could raise the price of a hotel room between them. No, they could not and the prospects looked bleak.

However all this changed when they reached Kleine Scheidegg. Rooms, food and baths were found for the heroes of the hour. The German Embassy in Bern loaded their celebration dinner with Nazi propaganda and there was an invitation to the Reichskanzlei to meet Adolf Hitler. As Heckmair dryly observed, 'From this there could be no escape.'

They went, of course, and had a face-to-face meeting with the man who was about to change the map of Europe and plunge the world into war. The dates of their climb were 21st–24th July, 1938. There is a book to be written some time on the real place that the rise of National Socialism and the Nazis played in the climbing of the Nordwands.

What is speculation is whether, without the enforced celebrations, Heckmair and Vörg might have gone on to France to tackle the unclimbed Walker Spur on the Grandes Jorasses. It was, after all, not many days later that the Italian Riccardo Cassin and his team did just this.

The first ascent of the Eiger Nordward was just too hard and serious for most climbers to comprehend. The war years took their toll and the second ascent was not made until 1947 by the great French guides and climbers Louis Lachenal and Lionel Terray. Steadily the best Alpine climbers took up the challenge and by 1957 there had been thirteen ascents.

No one had considered a winter ascent of this face yet. It was not until 1961 that the multi-talented Toni Hiebeler gathered his team of Anton Kinshofer, Andreas Mannhardt and Walter Almberger together with the very best equipment and clothing. Although they climbed it in two halves, using the gallery into the rail tunnel, they did the ascent in Alpine-style and stood the climbing world on its head.

This year also saw the first solo attempt when Adolf Mayr fell to his death. The next solo attempts were in 1962 when both Adolf Derungs and Diether Marchardt fell. The great Italian climber Walter Bonatti arrived in 1963 and climbed down safely but, starting the same day, Michel Darbellay showed class and completed the first solo in eighteen hours of climbing.

Loulou Boulaz had been on the face with Yvette Vaucher, but it was Daisy Voog, 'the Munich secretary' as the press dubbed her, who became the first woman to climb the face in 1964, when she was accompanied by Werner Bittner.

A face this vast with only two vertical routes was just too big a challenge to resist. The obvious unfinished direct start, pioneered by Sedlmayr and Mehringer, must have a direct finish. The best and most innovative climbers of the sixties started to probe, among the leaders of whom was American John Harlin. In 1965 he made a thorough reconnaissance with Dougal Haston and at last it seemed that things would start to happen.

The winter of 1966 saw an American and a German team battling it out for the Direct. In the end they co-operated but John Harlin was killed when a fixed rope he was jumaring on broke. The actual first ascent of what they called the Harlin route was made by Dougal Haston, Sigi Hupfauer, Jörg Lehne, Günther Strobel and Roland Votteler.

The first Alpine-style ascent of the Harlin route by Alex MacIntyre and Tobin Sorenson followed eleven years later and is one of the finest examples of inspired pure climbing talent in action. Since then the floodgates have opened and there are routes from one side to another. Some have become siege-bolted extravaganzas and others hard rock climbs with both difficult aid and free climbing available.

It was thirty years since the Eigerwand had submitted to its first successful solo ascent. Now it was my turn to return alone to that glorious face where I had participated in the fiftieth anniversary ascent of the original route. I would have two options – either to repeat my ascent of the 1938 route, or to break new ground and make an ascent on the Lauper side of the North Face.

From studying this face from mountains on the other side of the valley, there appeared to be a most obvious and logical line – a new moon-shaped arc curved its way majestically from the grassy slopes above Alpiglen to the final summit ridge. The line looked continuous – and if conditions were right, it would be possible to curve a way from base to summit, almost entirely on snow and ice, linking gaps through the various rock buttresses. So I had two options. Which I chose would depend upon the weather and conditions – we'd just have to wait and see.

I had hoped our summer in the Alps would improve my French and sketchy German, and that Tom and Kate might pick up a few words as well. But this proved to be far from the case. I used my French in the shops but through all the months in France the most common campsite tongue encountered was English. When we finally got to Switzerland, and walked through the streets of Grindelwald, Kate came out with an excellent 'Bonjour', but the German-speaking locals gave her such a glare that she was too discouraged to make much effort from then on!

Switzerland was awash with Dutch. Everywhere we turned Dutch tents and caravans would appear. Whilst camping in Zermatt and Grindelwald we never came across a single Frenchman, and later discovered that the French, although living next door, very rarely visit Switzerland. Germans were also much in evidence. But they, like the Dutch, spoke excellent English and were only too keen to use it, giving us little chance to practise!

All the same, it was great for Tom and Kate to have plenty of mates to play with on the campsites. The Dutch came well equipped for their holidays – big tents, big awnings and lots of enthusiasm and money to spend on téléphériques. With so much rain we were often camp-bound and having a variety of tents to circulate between seemed to help all the young families concerned! One extremely wet morning saw eight youngsters under Perkins' awning, all happily engrossed in colouring some pictures we had photocopied in large numbers before coming away! Japanese, Dutch, Germans alike, Tom and Kate were happy to mix; there were no barriers.

We arrived at the end of a short spell of good weather. Driving to Camping Eiger Nordwand, a site I remembered from my previous visits, we carefully negotiated Perkins into a suitable slot, watched over by the Chef d'Equipe, and proceeded to set up camp. It was *hot*! Too hot for anything and, as predicted by one of the locals, when temperatures rise quickly the weather breaks. It did – by teatime, as we were splashing in the coolness of the Grindelwald open-air pool, free to all people who stay in the village. A night of thunder, incredible lightning and torrential rain left some very wet and bedraggled holidaymakers and once more forced me to bide my time in patience. While the Eiger was totally out of condition I was able to take in a couple of training climbs on the Nollen Spur of the Mönch and the Jungfrau, but all I saw from these busy neighbouring tops was more bad weather creeping in from the south. And a temperature change after the heralded storm meant heavy fresh snow right down to 1300 metres. With the sun on it, it looked spectacular, but not like the Alps in July! We took damp family walks and picked enormous wild strawberries for tea.

Our resources, unlike the weather, were rapidly drying up. To pay for his new luxury toilet block the Chef d'Equipe was charging high rates. We considered our options. My other three climbs were in the Chamonix area, in the northern Dolomites and the southern Bregalia. To leave here would mean long and expensive journeys and an equally expensive return. In reality it would be cheaper to sit it out and wait for the good weather slot. We gritted our teeth and watched the campsite fill and empty as families gave up on the weather and moved on. In between showers we made the most of the Postbus network to gain height and enjoyed some wonderful family hikes on the grassy slopes around Grindelwald. As Tom, aged four, commented as he climbed well up into the clouds, 'Will we touch the sky?'

TUESDAY 20TH JULY

Rain!

WEDNESDAY 21ST JULY

Rain!

THURSDAY 22ND JULY

A mass exodus today – over half the campsite occupants have disappeared. Went for an early run up to Männlichen in the desperate hope that there might be sun above the clouds. Back to the mud and lunch.

Miraculously, as the cars and caravans disappeared, so did the clouds. Out came the sun – we could not believe it. Walking into town for a provision stock-up I had another peer at the old-fashioned weather station in the high street. It looked okay for Friday and Saturday.

The pattern of weather we had had was a warm day, a hot day, then a storm and immediately after, cold and wet weather before warming up again. The most recent storms had dumped a load of snow. Two dry days would mean a clear night in between and a breeze. The trick would be to get on the mountain before it melted off again. This idea was fine, but for days we had not seen the face.

Come what may, I decided to give it a whirl the next day.

JB: I carry the big rucksac down to the station. Alison walks hand in hand with the children. We have to see her off this time. The station is so busy and so many Japanese and Koreans want to photograph Kate that she has not the time to see and notice her mum leave.

Gradually, the afternoon rush quietens. We amble back to the campsite for tea.

FRIDAY 23RD JULY

Armed with a huge rucksac I boarded the early afternoon train, waved goodbye to my family and rode up the grassy slopes to Alpiglen.

Then taking a direct line up through the woods, I climbed up to the rocky shelves at the base of the face. I wanted to get as close as possible, but it needed to be a spot I could easily return to on my way down to Grindelwald after climbing the route. Also I wanted a flat place I could comfortably lie on and with plenty of water close at hand. I located a lovely grassy mound and wandered up behind to sort out a run-off from the face as a source of water.

With views down to the lights of Grindelwald I settled in for the evening. It was damp, swirling clouds still lurked, but above it was a clear starlit night. As I gazed out of the tight entrance of my Gore-Tex bivouac bag I watched shooting stars fall, and thought of the morrow.

SATURDAY 24TH JULY

Woke a couple of times in the night. The first time panic-struck to hear footsteps creeping up beside me. I sat up in fear, only to realise as it scampered away, that it was an inquisitive chamois sussing out the intruder.

After 4.00 a.m. I decided it was time to turn on the stove. No rush, I wanted natural light before I started the climbing proper. I began to prepare myself mentally.

JB: I set the alarm for 6.00 a.m. and got out of the tent carefully so as not to disturb the children. I sat at the set-up storage barrels and focused the Leitz binoculars on to the face. It was a cold sharp morning. I could see no one. Behind me another pair of binoculars was already in use. We conferred and went back to our beds. Alison was sticking to her plan. It looked like the weather was set for a wonderful day.

I packed the bivouac gear, sleeping bag, mat, stove, etc. into the big rucksac and the climbing gear for the route into a smaller light one, then carefully tied the big rucksac to a bush so that inquisitive cows could not nose it down the scree slopes.

Picking my way up the loose scree above, I negotiated a couple of small rock outcrops and so on to the base of the prominent snow slope that drops from the Hoheneis icefield.

JB: The Lauper route actually starts way to the right beneath the North Pillars and cuts across a ledge system from right to left. It crosses the base of the Hoheneis icefield by a long traverse left to where the old direct ascent for the impecunious to the Mittellegi Ridge went up. Then it curves back right to get above the Hoheneis and the foot of the key Lauper Gully.

Crampons on, Black Prophet tools out, my abseil rope firmly fastened in my rucksac – I was away.

Whilst a layer of fresh snow covered old dirty ice underneath, the top half of this narrow icy slope was cracked open with crevasses. After being forced right then back left, I negotiated my way to the very neck of the Hoheneis.

JB: It was 7.30 a.m. when I first saw Alison climbing. She was a small black spider romping up the steep ice; she disappeared from view as she climbed through the rocks that made up the neck of the Hoheneis, which itself looks like a head, but with three ears on its righthand side.

But the cold had not done the Hoheneis justice. Water still poured down the back in a huge cascade. Being unsporting enough not to want to get soaked at this stage I moved slightly right up a snowy ramp into a gully system. On precarious ground, fresh wet snow on rocky slabs and ledges, I headed up and then left above the neck of the Hoheneis. From here it was straight up. By climbing direct I had missed out the long traverse, left and then back right, of the Lauper route which avoids the Hoheneis and its snowy body.

I now looked at my route description to weigh up where that line would be coming in, and where to go next. Directly above me lay a fantastic vertical ice pitch falling from a snowy ledge. But as I watched it, it was collapsing and occasional huge spindrift avalanches would come streaming directly down the ice. Disappointed, I moved up, following a vague ramp and I was soon underneath and heading up into a huge funnel system coming down from the Mittellegi Ridge above. With the great solid rock buttress directly above me I traversed right and, moving up an unconsolidated and bottomless chimey, managed to get into an obvious gully leading straight on upwards.

The guide book talks about going right into a gully behind the great solid rock buttress . . .

JB: The children had wandered off to have breakfast with our German friends, the Hansen-Magnusson family, in their caravan. I explained to the line of Eiger/Alison-watchers that she would disappear behind the big rock buttress and probably not reappear for some time, up to the right where there is a ledge and a fine resting place. They wandered off for brews and late breakfasts, carefully securing their places by leaving binoculars, etc. on their seats.

Rike Hansen-Magnusson brought me wholemeal toast and a huge mug of hot coffee. I stood alone and idly looked at the face. A movement, tiny, caught my eye. Through the binoculars I could clearly see Alison climbing the mixed rock buttress to the left of the Lauper hidden key gully. Perhaps she needed a higher entry point?

No, she was climbing the buttress direct. It looked fantastic! Picking her way upwards, a move right, a move left, up, she was really pulling out the stops. The watchers scrambled back into place. Their knuckles were white. We were seeing history in the making. Alison was writing her talent on the greatest of the Alpine faces. She was creating a new climb, cutting up and left from the Lauper. Where would she go next? The toast and coffee were consumed cold.

I decided just to keep climbing. Moving up and left with the natural lie of the slope, through a tricky buttress overlaid with wet snow and ice, I carefully picked my way up and on. On the steep ice above I realised that the Mittellegi Ridge was starting to close from the left and I could see the hut way down below. I realised that I was heading straight up for the rock band that crosses the face horizontally from the right. I knew that the best way through on ice lay at its right-hand side.

So, climbing both up and right I reached a point where I could happily climb through. From here the climbing became good. The position was unrivalled and I was feeling great.

I knew that if I kept moving to avoid the inevitable deterioration of the ice as the temperature rose and the sun licked the face, I should be able to complete the climb and head for the summit.

JB: Watching her go through the rock band was great. The Lauper and Polish North Pillar route go through here. What would she do next? She stopped moving above the so-called Narrows and cut straight up. Once again breaking new ground. The children were unimpressed and could not see what all the fuss was about. It was just Mum climbing! Tom said he would have a look at her, when she was on top.

But the next section became a little tedious, now with better ice. The climbing, though still steep and spacey, became less absorbing and weariness started to creep in to my calves. As I climbed directly up, I could see way down to my right the ledge on the Lauper route and the base of the knobcrack.

My last obstacle was to be a triangular buttress spreading down and cutting off the face from the summit icefield.

Taking a gully directly above me on thin but good ice overlaying rock, I picked my way up and so on to the snowy arête that leads straight to the summit. 1.00 p.m. and I was finally there. I wanted to be pleased, but as I looked along the final summit ridge, my heart sank. With all the recent fresh snow and winds there were huge great meringue-like cornices spread about the ridge.

Always an unnerving proposition even as a roped pair, I knew that in being extra cautious and climbing well below the top of the ridge and the meringue cornices, traversing again on the steep ground would be very time consuming.

Kate: 'Dad, I want a poo!'

JB: So I missed her climbing the last steep section of the face. She climbed the last very steep section of the Lauper Direct Finish, first climbed by Erich Friedli and Ruedi Homberger, and actually topped out

at 12.55 p.m. Less than five and a half hours, a major new route and maybe the first climber to solo the North Face without wandering off to the Mittellegi Ridge. What an effort! She must be chuffed, and walking on air.

2.00 p.m. and the summit – at 3970 metres not my highest, but at least this time I could see for ever . . .

Not stopping for any refreshment, I felt a sense of urgency to get down. The fresh morning had rapidly turned into a hot day. The heat of the sun's rays was going to make for hideous conditions on the descent.

I set out, knocking off the snow balling up under my crampons at every step. The thick layer of fresh snow on the rock slabs was very unnerving. Occasionally I slid and would right myself.

The guidebook description for the descent of the West Ridge and South-west Flank talks about 'three red abseil points in place' down through a steeper gully section. As I found what I assumed to be the top one, I got out my ropes for the first and only time, happy to feel secure for a few metres. On arrival at the bottom end of my ropes there were no more red abseil points. I realised that the top two must have been buried in deep snow. I coiled my ropes and set off once again.

I came to the top of a steep gully, peered cautiously down and tried to weigh up my safest means of descent. I did not want to head too far left as that would take me on to the rocks above the glacier. Rightwards was extremely steep. But I knew I had to get to the base of that gully. There were faint signs of footprints way below. So, picking my way carefully down, crampons cutting through the snow and slush on to the rocks beneath, I zig-zagged left and right and finally to the base of the gully.

The footprints were obvious now in an upward direction and it was reassuring to know that recently someone else had been on the mountain.

The angle eased off a little and as I descended left I came across something blue lying in the snow. It turned out to be a Gore-Tex jacket. I smiled at the thought that, of all the things I needed, being sponsored by Sprayway, I should find a jacket! I took off my rucksac and threaded it through the lid.

I was now heading right and then back left, following a natural line that I could vaguely pick out.

75

Five or maybe ten minutes later and there below me was something else lying in the snow – a headtorch and an empty packet of biscuits, at which I laughed. The birds round here do not miss a trick! Lying further down was a waistbag. As I picked it up I realised it was full of loose change and when I unzipped it, the wallet was stuffed full of Spanish peseta notes! This was clearly not discarded gear. Either I would come across someone looking for it, or I would have to hand it in to the police. Once more sticking the oddments in my rucksac I set off down again trying to weigh up the circumstances that would make someone drop a jacket. Well, that was easy; had it just been tucked under a rucksac lid, it could easily have dropped out. But to lose a waistbag, headtorch and a packet of biscuits – that was a bit more mysterious.

As I continued to negotiate the slope I came to the conclusion that a climber had slipped. His rucksac pocket had been open, some bits had fallen out; his fall on such terrain had taken him a fair distance down, and he was too shaken or weary to go back for his kit.

Only a few seconds after reaching this conclusion yet more kit appeared. This time a brand-new harness, half pulled out of the bag that contained it, a single crampon and a pair of Gore-Tex over-trousers. Once more loaded up, I worried about the scenario. Would I catch up with the chap struggling down or would I never see him again?

As I traversed right on a big broken ledge under a steep section of the rock, I suddenly spotted two figures, way down on the glacier. (Later they turned out to have been two totally uninvolved people heading dangerously late up the Western Flank.)

As they were sitting next to a tiny track through the snow I was unsure in which direction they were moving, but I felt that finally I had spotted the missing link. So there had been two. Obviously one had slipped, gone quite some way but not returned back up to collect the gear. For some unknown reason they had continued straight on down; maybe one had broken an arm?

Still following the easiest line I traversed back down left, then below an extremely steep gully saw something shiny. What now! Nervously I debated whether to climb down and sort it out, or just to continue down. It was obviously more gear and did I want to be bothered carrying it all anyway?

Cautiously, I turned in to face the slope and climbed down. A karabiner clipped into a titanium ice screw and above it an ice axe with a glove still pushed through the hand leash. I shuddered as I imagined the fall, and at the thought of someone desperately trying to keep hold of the axe – only to have his hand slide out of the glove. I sat down, took out a drink, thought for a moment and then, rucksac heavily laden once more, the axe on the back, started down again.

I was getting closer now. Eigergletscher Station was well visible and I could see people pottering around and up on to the edge of the glacier. Moving rightwards on to the rocky section of the West Flank, I started to pick up cairns – I had nearly cracked it. Just one more wide right sweeping traverse across the rocks, back left and then down to the glacier and home.

I had started to sing gently to myself and now felt like whooping for joy. Suddenly from somewhere within me I felt a voice. *No, not yet.* Assuming it to be my inner cautious self telling me not to celebrate until back on safe ground, I carried on, unalarmed but quietly, along the rocky track through the buttress.

I turned a corner and was just about to descend a wee chimney when, across to my left, something caught my eye again. More gear, this time a red rucksac. I contoured across towards it and then I realised, not only was there a rucksac, all empty and ripped, but a body still attached to it; a man, his big mountain boots still fastened to his feet, lay contorted below me.

The little rock step I was on had had a small overhang, as his head, if there still was one, was tucked underneath and out of sight. I had no wish to go down and check how he would look; his eyes would haunt me for ever.

There was no need to check if he was still alive. I knew instantly that he was dead; the way he lay, the colour of his body, his half-naked chest, lightly clad, his clothes ripped and shredded. There was no movement, no sound. I tried to estimate the distance he had fallen. He must have bounced down, down and down until reaching this flat section of rock where he had come to rest.

I sat down and wept. Maybe normally I might have handled it, but on this instance I was tired, mentally and physically. I cried and cried until my sorrows finally shook me into some sense. But what was I to do? There was no way I could take this man down on my own. To fetch help would mean having to leave him. That felt wrong – I felt I owed it to him to get him safely off the mountain. But how?

Then an idea and reason. If I could see and vaguely hear people down at Eigergletscher Station, it was not unreasonable to assume I could attract attention. I started to wave and shout. Shout and wave. Then exhausted with the senselessness of it all, sat down and wept again.

When I was calm I stood up and returned to waving my arms. Then success! Over the col from behind the Jungfrau appeared a helicopter, heading in the right direction. My waves got more frantic and I cried with excitement and relief. But the chopper was not coming my way. It continued on a straight course, over Eigergletscher and down towards Grindelwald. I sat for a few moments and assumed it would be turning. It didn't. Yet again I burst into tears. This was futile. Down at Eigergletscher I thought I could see people gathering, looking. But where was the helicopter?

I listened. Then the gentle trickle of a meltwater stream – a sound that would become a reminder for ever – gave way to the distant sound of helicopter blades, and from over the ridge below me came a helicopter flying straight to Eigergletscher. I jumped up and down with excitement – they had seen me after all! Tears flowed with relief.

Momentarily my heart sank, as the helicopter turned and landed beside the railway track. There was a lot of activity going on down there. People in orange suits were getting out with kit, then once again, the rotors were humming and it was heading up the glacier, then slowly ascending the mountainside, facing in. They were obviously looking for something – but had not spotted me.

I stood up and waved frantically as the helicopter came up from behind the rock buttress below me. The nose of the red machine rose up in front of me and I could see the masked and ear-muffed pilot and observer. The force of the rotor blades blasted meltwater everywhere. I covered my eyes and waved, indicating the body below. In acknowledgement they nodded, rose up directly above me, and a well-equipped mountain guide came sliding down from inside the helicopter.

He put his arms around me, as if to console me, I thought. But he was pumping my right arm and shaking my hand. 'Wunderbar, wunderbar,' he was shouting above the noise of the helicopter.

I stood confused. Then I remembered that earlier that morning a solitary helicopter had flown past the North Face and crossed the Mittellegi Ridge. Presumably someone had seen me and now he was congratulating me on my ascent. But all that mattered to me was the contorted wreck of a man I had been standing guard over for the past half hour; it seemed much, much longer. All I wanted was for him and me to get out of there.

My new friend finally acknowledged the body and in broken English shouted, 'We will take you down.' Another man was lowered beside us. He too shook me by the hand, and then proceeded to inspect the position of the body; he was a police officer. Down came the cable again and up I went next.

Down at Eigergletscher I started to detune, taking off my harness and waterproof suit, opening my rucksac to empty the contents on to the floor into two piles. I knew exactly what was mine. Something inside me just wanted to get rid of the rest. As I stuffed my own gear back into my sac, deep in thought, I became aware of a tall dark climber walking up the path. It was a bit late in the day for climbers to be still around.

I tried to talk to him, uttering my few words of Spanish; but he spoke no English or French, so we gave up. Then he saw the pile of gear and clothes. With two Portuguese workers from the station trying to translate, I tried to explain. I desperately wanted to be able to tell him what had happened but couldn't break bad news in mime and gestures. Then events cut his suspense brutally short. The Swiss doctor's radio buzzed. 'They are bringing the body down now,' she said. Seconds later the helicopter was overhead and underneath it, hung on a wire, spinning gently round, was the big solid horizontal bag.

The Spanish lad looked up and burst into tears. I wanted to console him. But how? I felt upset and useless. Numbly, I promised the policeman who had been on the mountain that I would call at the police station in Grindelwald next day to make a statement.

As I talked to the stationmaster, waiting for the train, the sequence of events soon became clear. The two Spanish climbers had set off up the West Flank of the Eiger fairly early that morning after a bivouac near to Eigergletscher. As they climbed Francisco had become increasingly tired and started to lag behind, so they decided that Juan Carlos should continue alone whilst Francisco would have a rest, then descend to wait at Eigergletscher for Juan Carlos' return. The day passed and by 3.30 p.m. he was concerned enough to request a routine helicopter check.

Meanwhile Juan Carlos had continued to climb. In the increasing heat he shed his Gore-Tex jacket and overtrousers and put them under the lid of his rucksac. When he slipped and fell, he had bounced down the West Flank, his rucksac catching on protruding rocks and he had shed his gear in the way I had found it.

By now the helicopter, pilot, assistant, guide, policeman and doctor had disappeared. The last train down was due in half an hour. Francisco and I waited and went down to Grindelwald together.

As I walked into the campsite it was 7.30 p.m. I felt in need of affection. There was no one there. So dumping my rucksac and feeling conspicuous in heavy mountain boots, I walked over to the new toilet block. No one. I went out to the children's playground. Tom and Kate were engrossed on the rope roundabout. I sat on the wall to watch, not wanting to disturb them, but longing for a cuddle.

JB: I last saw Alison about half past one as she disappeared near the summit. After lunch I took the children to the open-air swimming baths and expected to find her back around 5.00 p.m. at the latest. However we had spoken about her staying up at Kleine Scheidegg if she was tired and coming down in the morning. After tea, I washed up whilst the children played and I was surprised to see Alison's rucksac outside the tents when I returned.

Tom spotted me, leapt down and charged across to hug me. Kate seeing her brother leap off wondered what all the excitement was about and she came and joined Tom and me. We walked back to the tents together to meet JB.

Next day JB, Tom, Kate and I, with the friendly Hansen-Magnussons, caught the train to Alpiglen and had a great time retracing my steps to my bivouac spot to recover the rest of my gear before wandering in the rain through the woods back to Grindelwald.

That afternoon I called at the police station to make my statement.

I rested for a few days and after a steady drive through Switzerland and a huge stock-up shop down the valley, we returned once more to Chamonix.

8

CHAMONIX INTERLUDE

The mountains are on fire.

Tom Ballard, 4½

The weather was great by the standard of the spring and early summer. But so too was the quantity of people in Chamonix. Packed out, it was all a bit much. The campsites were chock-a-block and on Friday the queue of cars and caravans from one campsite disappeared down the road, further than the eye could see. Winding gradually back into rock climbing again, we visited the valley crags and, moving from car park to car park, peacefully escaped the crowds and conserved money.

The North Face of the Petit Dru receives little sun until late afternoon and stubbornly remained plastered in snow and ice. The Niche snowfield was not getting any smaller and still came far enough down to cover some of the key rock pitches.

Checking up on the weather forecast in Les Houches, we bumped into Ian 'Spike' Sykes, a good friend in the ski equipment business in Scotland. He had mislaid his car and we helped him retrieve it. The children were ecstatic at the unexpected arrival of Uncle Pike and even more so when he offered to feed them chips and ice cream, luxuries they had not indulged in for nearly five months! As Spike drove us back to our designated spot for the night (a car park under the Gaillards) and negotiated the obstacles of Chamonix, we distracted him with teases about the luxury of having a *reverse* gear.

We had been enjoying the fruits of the valley, literally, picking wild bilberries behind the crag in Les Houches and wild raspberries in the woods of Les Bois. Now it was time for me to get some classic Alpine rock routes done in order to limber up for my next assault on the big ones. With the valley so horribly busy, we decided to go higher up into the mountains and give Tom and Kate their first experience of bivouacking.

As everyone who has done it knows, going away for one night requires as much kit as going away for six!

Unfortunately when going away with children the quantities required are not linear – going for a bivouac with two children for one night feels like carrying gear for six!

For a night out in the mountains there was just no way we could cut down easily. The children, and we, had to be warm. First of all, each required a sleeping bag, a good down-filled one, and even compressed this took up nearly a rucksac! We decided to share a child apiece in the bivvi bags, and so with two Gore-Tex ones stuffed in, it was time to plan food. Normally on a bivouac I'm fairly frugal with food, not wanting to carry a load of weight, knowing I can easily cope and survive with something in the valley to look forward to. But with youngsters it was different; Tom and Kate would need feeding well, and at the higher, colder altitude even more so; we'd have to take plenty of it.

As I worked out the meals for two days and nights the pile started to mount up! Biscuits, eggs, milk, cereal, hot chocolate, sugar, spare clothes, spare nappies; you name it, we took it. After having our enormous sacs and hand bags stolen we were restricted to a number of small sacs, and with having to carry Kate, it was to be long uphill work!

Following a night and morning of rain we packed far more food and equipment than we could really carry and, catching the cable car to La Flégère, set off up into the mountains of the Aiguilles Rouges. Katie ambled slowly along beside JB and me as we struggled with all the kit, while Tom marched sturdily off into the distance with a French lad and his dad, only to be seen again at Lac Blanc. Finding a safe yet scenic spot, we dressed Tom and Kate in all their spare clothes, loaded them into down sleeping bags and bivouac bags and settled down for a bone-cold night.

We woke at dawn to watch the sun light up Mont Blanc. A very frosty start left a layer of ice on the bivouac bags, but in the most beautiful sunny morning that followed, the children amused them-selves on compact snow patches, while I disappeared to make a fine rock climb up the South Arête Intégrale of the Aiguille de la Persévérance (2901m), down the West Arête and up to the East Ridge of the Aiguille des Chamoix (2902m). A fast descent down old snow gullies and I was soon back with the family.

Next day dawned cloudy. After a leisurely breakfast we explored the shores of the Lac Blanc, and on the way down I climbed the Southeast Arête of the Aiguille de l'Index (2595m) before we descended back to La Flégère and Perkins.

The rest of the week remained unsettled, with hot afternoons and/or mornings, when it would usually deteriorate to showers or storms. I was still keen to make an attempt on the North Face of the Dru but feared these showers would not be helping clear the lower shady rock cracks of ice.

I kept fit on the rocks of Les Gaillands. By now Tom and Kate were getting very adept at playing climbing. Wherever there were bolts near the bottom they were able to do a route, borrowing slings of all widths, colours and lengths to make harnesses, then clipping on a few karabiners and setting off. Tom's idea of a great route was to have a long series of slings linked together and clipped into a bolt with a karabiner above him, the other end clipped into him below. By leaping around and lifting his feet off the floor he was able to part climb up the slings and part dangle in space – great fun but questionable ethics! Imitating other paired climbers, they were quite keen to 'help' me by feeding out the rope from below, but seeing as they usually lost concentration within thirty seconds and then were more likely to tug down on the rope, it was help I unsportingly discouraged! If there were little boulders then they loved to imitate bouldering, Kate's over-enthusiasm and lack of fear causing me much anxiety as an over-protective mum! But if they had gear to play with, and this included occasional experiments with huge mountain boots and crampons, the clinking and colours all added to the reality. I would often return from a long run or a climb and Kate would ask unconcernedly, 'Have you been up the mountains?', and when I said yes, 'Which one?' she'd ask and I'd point, even if she was none the wiser!

After a few days some friends, Steve and Alex Holland, arrived from the UK. Chamonix was choked and hot – they were away for some relaxation and were not going to get it there. We swopped tales of the summer's activities and made plans for our next move. Tom and Kate were ecstatic; Grandma and Grandpa had done them proud, and as Steve and Alex unpacked out came a bag full of goodies . . . new desert boots for the pair of them, new sandals and new wellies, colouring books and crayons, some of Grandma's excellent knitting, and an extra supply of sheets and towels! So everyone was happy. Tomorrow we'd leave the chaos. Chamonix had been our meeting point, but it was only a stopover, Saturday would see us rolling south for the delights and ice creams of Italy!

9

PIZ BADILE – 3308m

A great climb marred by tragedy.

Riccardo Cassin

The curving North Ridge and magnificent North Face of the Piz Badile can be clearly seen from the old road between Bondo and Promonto. They are just finishing a beautifully engineered new road that will completely bypass these villages and make them even more pleasant to explore. The name Piz Badile means mountain shovel, and indeed the entire North Face does look like an enormous shovel blade, the summit being where the handle would go!

The first ascent of the Piz Badile, then called Cima di Tschingel, was made by W.A.B. Coolidge with François and Henri Devouassoud in 1867. They climbed what is now the South Face descent route, from the Baths of Masino above San Marino. In 1892 Christian Klucker made a solo attempt on the obvious and appealing North Ridge. There followed many attempts on the ridge, some using dubious tactics, until it was finally climbed in 1923 by Walter Risch and Alfred Zürcher (who went on to make the first ascent of the Lauper route, on the North Face of the Eiger).

The unclimbed North Face of Piz Badile now beckoned. The challenge was taken up by various Italian parties without success until 1937. In July of that year the great Riccardo Cassin (first ascent of the Walker Spur, Grandes Jorasses), Gino Esposito and Vittorio Ratti were biding their time in the Sciora Hut, waiting for the area's notoriously violent storms to abate. Sheltering in the hut outhouse was a rival pair, Mario Molteni and Giuseppe Valsecchi. Eventually, both teams began climbing, taking two different starts. They climbed

The Cassin route on the North Face
of the Badile (3308m)

NORTH RIDGE

steadily throughout the day and as Cassin and his party were setting up their bivouac they were joined by Molteni and Valsecchi.

The next morning Molteni asked if they could climb as a roped team of five. Cassin reluctantly agreed and on they climbed. They had a hard day and it was a tired team who started to prepare their second bivouac at 9.00 p.m. The weather was getting worse and Cassin was concerned about the physical strength of Molteni and Valsecchi. A violent storm erupted and soon they were all soaked to the skin. The storm passed, the sky cleared and the temperature fell. By morning they needed to climb on, if only to warm up. They found the climbing hard and after a couple of hours Molteni and Valsecchi were having difficulty in keeping up and needed continual assistance. Needless to say the weather started to worsen and by lunchtime it began to rain. The temperature started to drop. Cassin records what happened next: 'The rain changed to hail: our faces were lashed by hailstones, while the icy wind froze our soaked arms and legs. Suddenly the hail stopped and it began to snow, plastering the face. We had to reach the top at all costs: a bivouac on the face in those conditions could be fatal to us all.'

They made their summit at 4.00 p.m., but the struggle was only just beginning. 'Lightning snaked around us and we were white with ice.' More seriously, the condition of Molteni and Valsecchi was deteriorating rapidly.

We did everything possible to ward off the death that was stalking us: we poured all our cognac between Molteni's lips; I tried to support him when he no longer had the strength to continue, but in vain. Without so much as a moan he sank to the ground, never to rise again.

We stopped for a moment in silence. Our feelings demanded that we take poor Molteni's remains with us and, for a moment, emotion defeated reason: loading him on my shoulders, I tried to go on down, but the effort was super-human in those uncontrolled elements. On the advice of Esposito, who had stayed to help me, I tucked the body by a boulder, to shelter it a bit from the storm.

We then joined Ratti and Valsecchi, who were unaware of the tragedy. We said nothing to Valsecchi, so as not to upset him too much in his disastrous condition. But when an unexpected difficulty blocked the way and we bunched up, Valsecchi looked for Molteni and, not seeing him, guessed what had happened.

Standing near a boulder, he wept silently. Suddenly, he dropped to the ground. In vain we held him up, trying to shake him out of the torpor which had invaded him but he too, without a word, was left lifeless in our arms.

There was nothing for the survivors to do but endure their third bivouac and in the morning carry Valsecchi's body down the mountain.

We had been on the face for fifty-two hours, climbing for thirty-four and for twelve hours the storm had lashed us without respite. Next day we went back up the Badile with the rescue team which had come up from the valley to recover our friends' bodies.

What a climb, what conditions. We must all feel admiration for the way Cassin and his team stood by their unlooked-for companions and made sure their remains were recovered. There is much modern professional climbing can learn from past masters.

The second ascent was made in poor weather, with two awful bivouacs, by Gaston Rébuffat and Bernard Pierre in 1949. The climb's classic reputation was made. Climbers from around the world were drawn to the magnificent granite slabs and the challenging quality of the climbing.

In 1952 Hermann Buhl, the most talented climber of his generation and one of the greatest climbers of all time, cycled into Bondo, and walked up to the face. 'I wriggled, heaved and straddled myself up the face.' He had soloed the route in just four and a half hours. The climbing world was stunned!

Winter climbing in the area is a rare and precious thing. In December 1967, Michel Darbellay, who made the first solo ascent of the 1938 route on the Eiger, arrived with Daniel Troillet and Camille Bournissen from Switzerland at the same time as the Italian team of Alessandro Gogna (first solo ascent Walker Spur, Grandes Jorasses), Paolo Armando and Gianni Calcagno. They united and fixed ropes from a snow cave at the foot of the face, went home for Christmas when the weather broke and returned to continue unfinished business on 29th December. They pressed on and topped out on 2nd January, 1968. Over the years more rock routes have been introduced on the face, so that in good weather the face can now be climbed in scores of places. But the tiny glacier under the face has dried out so much that it is nearly impassible and the North Face and its climbs have to be approached from the foot of the North Ridge.

My knowledge of the Bregaglia region was minimal. I had only really heard of the Piz Badile and had only seen photographs of it in magazines, so had little idea what to expect. It was seventy years since the great and fine ascent of the fabulous North Ridge and now I was hoping to do a solo on the great classic of the North Face – the Cassin route.

The campsite belonging to the tiny village of Bondo in the southern Bregaglia could not have been more different from Chamonix. It was a large flat field with a mobile loo in a corner and a water trough running down one side. During the winter, they told us, the field was flooded to provide a local skating rink. Although the facilities were very basic, the campsite was clean and wholesome, while after the chaos of Chamonix in season the unspoilt village of Bondo was idyllic. We could collect fresh milk, yoghurt, eggs and cheese from the local co-operative, a place so clean you could have eaten off the floor, and we could swim and bathe in the icy river tumbling down from the glaciers above.

Another difference for us was that our family camping unit had been enlarged by one hundred per cent! As well as the good company of Steve and Alex, who had driven with us from Chamonix, we enjoyed the reappearance of Spike with another old Scottish friend, Ian 'Suds' Sutherland. They had come to the Bregaglia to do a warm-up rock route before tackling the Matterhorn. It was great to have their company over a vast evening pasta as we all discussed the weather forecast and our various plans for the next day.

I went for an afternoon run to take a closer look at the Piz Badile's North Face. The sunny day turned to a torrential storm, and, as I ran higher, I had some incredible views of no fewer than five waterfalls cascading down the face in impressive white columns.

I decided to go up to the foot of the face next day, but could see it would not be a place to take the children. Steve came with me to the Sciora Hut where we met up with Spike and Suds who had returned from a great day's climbing on the Flat Iron.

After we set up our tents near a plentiful supply of glacial spring water, I headed across the rock-strewn slope to try and get an idea of the approach to the North Face. As I climbed up, over and round boulders towards the glacier beneath the face, I came across three wild-looking Czechs camping beside a swollen meltwater stream. They proudly announced that they were waiting for two friends to return from the North Face and lent me their binoculars to look at the climbers bivouacking on a ledge on the right of a col on the skyline ridge.

The weather forecast was good for the morrow and worse for the day after, so I began to consider going for it next day instead of doing a training route with Steve as originally planned. Steve was generous about this. My climb had to come first he said.

THURSDAY IOTH AUGUST

I did not sleep well. The tent was on a slope, I was unsure of the weather and my granite-slab-climbing technique was rusty. Although I had solo climbed the Big Three, I still had not solo climbed a big long rock route.

6.00 a.m. and the sky was clearing. I leapt out of my sleeping bag and shot down to the Sciora Hut to look at the météo station. The pressure was steady. Tomorrow the forecast was even better – but what if it changed?

I nipped back up to the MSR stove and over breakfast Steve and I discussed the weather. I decided to go. As briskly as possible I motored round towards the ridge leading down from the North Ridge proper.

By 8.30 a.m. I was at the pass and changing my sweat-drenched shorts and tee shirt for a dry tee shirt and trousers. Then, leaving my sleeping bag, food and ski poles under a boulder, I set off.

As I arrived, Spike and Suds, after a comfy night at the Sciora Hut, were changing into rock boots. I did likewise and followed them up the first easy section of their climb to a col at the base of the North Ridge proper.

We chatted and exchanged photographs. Then saying au revoir, I headed down a ramp to traverse across to the start of the North Face.

First I had to cross a huge plug of old snow left on the ledge after the winter. My problem was how to get off it in smooth-soled rock boots and with only a light ice axe. Behind the snow plug the ice had melted away from the rock leaving a large gap. The top of the plug was well away from the rock and overhung.

I dug in the ice axe on its outer side and lowered myself, back to the rock, carefully down the other side into the gap. Kicking footholds in the snow was no fun in rock boots until I could reach across to the rock on the far side. Then a foothold collapsed and as I slid down on to the weight of my arms, outstretched from the ice axe, my chest slid down the spike on the axe's shaft. Desperately, I kicked into the snow again, saving myself from falling down into the void, a depth I was unsure of, and finally straddled across to the rock.

Shaken and in pain, I dried my boots and wobbled over the rest of the ramp, grateful for having taken *one* axe but cursing not having a pair of ice tools and a pair of crampons!

Up the easy cracks to the base of the first dièdre. Some Isostar and Frusli. Then, well after 10.00 a.m., it was time to get going.

I took out the route description and weighed up exactly which of the corners above I was supposed to climb. The guide talked about 'a well-pegged open-book dièdre'. I could see what I thought must be the right line, but what I could not see were any pegs! I counted the grooves and corners across the face and, matching those to the route description in my hand, decided that really was it.

From below it looked awkward and difficult but, once established, I started to enjoy the solid feel of the rock as I jammed up the crack with hands and fingers, using positive holds for my feet. From here the route went diagonally left up fine solid cracks to another dièdre.

Here I came across the first of the parties I was to pass that day, slowly picking their way above the second dièdre. Pausing for a moment to work out the moves, the rock overhung above me and was undercut beneath me. I teetered left, then up, and so towards the Czech team, wearing antiquated red nylon cagoules. They seemed delighted at my arrival and, encouraged by their congratulations and warmth of friendship, I climbed on up the delicate slabs above.

Once again I was behind another party, this time a lad and a girl whom I had seen back at the campsite yesterday. Her welcome was not endearing and I waited a while for her leader to make himself safe after the next pitch. I said my 'excuse me's and passed on by. As I reached the point that I assumed to be the site of one of Cassin and his party's bivouacs, I once more consulted my route description. Then, on pleasant slabby cracks, once more traversed up and left to reach what was called the Snowpatch. This feature in the central part of the face has gradually receded over the years with dry summers and poor winters and was now only really visible as a loose pile of frost-broken rocks. Way over to my left I heard the whine and then the crash of stonefall, and I stood a moment to ensure none was heading my way.

Above the Snowpatch the rock steepens, a slabby pitch leading into a steep corner, a chimney and a flake crack. Above me were two more climbing teams, two people just setting out on the top crack and soon to head out of sight, but below them a team of three who seemed to be having problems. Finding a suitable ledge, I took off my rucksac and sat down to have a drink and weigh up what was going on ahead of me.

The leader had finished climbing and was belayed above the chimney. His second man was just about to enter the steep section round the chimney and the third man was starting to climb. Not long to wait – or so I hoped. But as the second man thrashed, grunted and shouted it became obvious that he was less than happy; whilst his activity rate was high, his progress was not very upward and his mate looked a touch embarrassed! A lot of shouting, a lot of waiting (getting on for an hour) and finally he was out and up, presumably having jammed himself and his rucksac in the chimney and having had to sort out a way to overcome his problem.

I waited until the third man was well clear of the chimney and set about it myself. Steep but positive crack climbing, it reminded me of the great classic, Green Crack, on the gritstone edge of Froggatt in Derbyshire, only the other way round, and, careful not to jam myself likewise, I negotiated the undercut holds beneath the roof, round the corner and up. The three-man team was still on the ledge and happy to let me pass by. I steamed on past and into the next flake and groove system.

The angle eased off again now and after another pitch of pleasant slab climbing, a traverse led left to overlook a great couloir sweeping down to my left and the glacier below. Then on, up easier ground to a fine ledge and the two-man team perched on it. From here the route was obvious; a fine flake and crack line leading upwards and right. Easily I followed the crack and then it turned into a corner chimney. Jamming one foot and hand in the snowy crack at the back I continued my upward progress. The chimney got wider now and whilst for a time I was able to use both side walls, I soon had to make a choice as to which side seemed best. The whole of the back wall was streaming with water which, as I reached my arms above my head, proceeded to stream down me; I was getting soaked! But it was not a problem; I knew I was near my goal and it would not stop me now.

Some tricky moves over a roof at the back of the gully and I was at the place where the Cassin original line crossed left and required an abseil into a couloir system and so to the top.

My decision was to finish direct by following a slightly harder yet more straightforward and logical line. Following the chimney line for a couple more metres, I picked up a leftward diagonal line of flakes and traversed across up on to an airy little nose of rock.

From here I could see the summit only fifty metres above. Just below the top I could pick out the two figures of the last team in front of me. Weighing up the next sequence of moves, I worked carefully up the rock. It was a beautiful pitch, absorbing climbing on fine granite slabs 800 metres from the glacier at the base of the climb – I was thoroughly enjoying it. As I moved from the slabs in a series of flakes and blocks that led to the ridge, I caught up with the two Swiss boys I had seen earlier. Elated at their own ascent, but also genuinely pleased for mine, they shook me by the hand and congratulated me. To coincide with my arrival the clouds fell and we were enveloped in a damp mist. I wondered about the other two teams, both still on the face below . . .

We decided to team up for the descent and used both our sets of ropes for abseils, with some very rapid down-climbing between. We were soon well down the North Ridge.

As we dropped through the mist, which had brought out the lichen on the rock in a luminous green/yellow glow, we caught up with Suds and Spike on their descent. Back at the col we put our ropes away and said our cheerios. The Swiss boys had offered me a celebratory beer, but they were returning to the Sciora Hut, for more climbing, so we had to part company as I descended through the woods and steep slopes, past the Sass Fura Hut, down to the quiet pastures of Bondo.

JB: Alex was out walking with the children when Suds and Spike appeared, hot, sweaty, but excited. 'She's done it!' Suds yelled. 'She's okay and she's on her way.'

Alex starts off up the approach path and I put the stoves on. Alison arrives hot and bubbling. I prepare the regulation megapasta for all, and countless brews, while Alex takes Alison to the river to show her a pool to swim and wash in. It must have been freezing. What a great night. The children drop asleep in our arms and the adults talk into the early hours. Bondo is such an amazing contrast to the fleshpots of Cham.

Next day Spike and Suds set off for Zermatt and the Matterhorn and we indulged in a relaxing day around Bondo. Tom and Kate scrambled among the water-polished granite boulders by the riverside, we swam in clean icy pools and picked wild raspberries to go with the local yoghurt for tea. Steve and Alex headed off to visit a friend in Leysin and I had time to calculate how best to complete the last two of my Big Six in the three weeks I had at my disposal before I had to be in Munich for Sprayway at the ISPO trade show.

We were close to Italy, so the logical thing to do would have been to drive over to the Dolomites, spend some time getting used to the rock, and climb the Comici route on the Cima Grande di Lavaredo. Then we would have to drive back to Chamonix to finish off with the Dru. But after the recent sunny weather the Dru should be in condition right now. If September began stormy, it could easily go out of condition again. I didn't want to risk missing the right moment, and if I did the Dru straight away, there was a good chance I could still fit in the Cima Grande before Munich. How much better to go off there with my tally complete and knowing I didn't have to get back into serious soloing mode again afterwards. So my decision was made. It was Friday the 13th and the Dru was calling. We packed our bags and headed back to work.

10

THE DRU – 3733m

The Drus are an unblemished mountain. In appearance they are the very epitome of the imagin-
ary mountain, of one single upthrust of naked rock.

Guido Magnone

The Drus are easily visible from the Chamonix valley and the West
Face of the Petit Dru is a favourite if formidable view from Montenvers at the top of the rack railway. There are two summits, the
Grand Dru (3754m) and the Petit Dru (3733m), separated by a small
gap, the Brèche des Drus. Both summits were first climbed in the late
1870s, and the first winter ascent was a traverse of both in 1928. The
impressive West Face of the Petit Dru was discounted as a blank
impossibility and attention turned to its northern aspect.

The skills called for to master the North Face of the Petit Dru were
the newly evolving techniques of the free rock climber, and one of the
leading exponents in the 1930s was Parisian climber Pierre Allain, who
developed his art on the famous boulders of Fontainebleau. (The well-
known rock boots known as PAs were his invention.) He had
difficulty at first finding a suitable partner for the Petit Dru, but
eventually teamed up with Raymond Leininger. Meanwhile a party of
four Swiss guides, led by the formidable Raymond Lambert, got in
first and climbed as far as the Niche, a patch of never-melting snow set
like a waymark halfway up the face.

Allain and Leininger rushed over to the Alps that same summer and
on 31st July 1935 they had their chance. With just one bivouac, they
reached the summit on 1st August. Never small-minded, Allain
acknowledged the awkward nature of what became known as the

The Allain route on the North Face
of the Petit Dru (3733m)

NICHE

Fissure Lambert. Subsequent climbers have found the Fissure Allain hard going too, without aid, and have worked out various alternatives to avoid it.

After the Second World War the focus of attention on the Petit Dru shifted to the challenge of the sheer West Face, though new routes were still being added to the North Face and it became popular with the leading names of winter climbing from all over Europe.

In the past the normal route of approach was to flog steeply uphill to the bottom of the Dru from the Mer de Glace opposite Montenvers. However in more recent years a recognised, and more acceptable, approach has been to take the Grands Montets téléphérique up to its top station, then contour south and west to descend a gully which arrives above the glaciers at the base of the Nant Blanc Face of the Aiguille Verte. From these you descend towards the base of the North Face of the Dru. It is for this reason alone that I have never before climbed on the Dru! I never fancied the idea of a slog up from Montenvers and, as most of my previous Alpine trips had been out of season when the user-friendly mechanical uphill transports are closed, I always left the Dru for another day.

The appearance of the Dru is splendid, not so much as a mountain but as a beautifully sculptured form in rock. It has always had a special appeal for me. On my second visit to the Alps, Ian Parsons and I accumulated a series of fine rock routes, but in more recent years I have tended to stay away from the classic rock climbs that Chamonix has to offer, tending more to the great Alpine faces. So for this reason, I had got out of practice at the techniques and skills desirable for the most enjoyable ascents on Chamonix granite. A friend remarked that he had talked to an early climber who had vivid memories of hideous chimneys and cracks. This concentrated the mind!

I read the route description in Gaston Rébuffat's *The Mont Blanc Massif: the 100 Finest Routes* and kept reading his comment that an ascent of the North Face of the Petit Dru was best attempted by a team well used to awkward Chamonix cracks. The harsh granite forms beautifully sculptured flakes, cracks and pinnacles. However without the skill to negotiate them, I knew they might prove problematic!

The first solo of the North Face was made only twenty-three years ago. It has never become a popular route on solo climbers' tick lists so the number of ascents has been very few. Of the classic six north faces it is probably one of the least popular to solo, and as I prepared myself it was easy to see why!

Perkins and the family were back in Chamonix. It was August and le Weekend – very busy and very hot. After the peace and tranquillity of Bondo, it was all a bit too much.

I had had enough of living out of Perkins, however charming he was! It was still Saturday morning, a changeover for holidaymakers, so maybe we would be able to find a spot at a site? Once more, we returned to the quiet of Les Drus campground and found a pitch into which we could negotiate Perkins.

The météo forecast said thundery and changeable until Tuesday, but then a little better! We bouldered, sunbathed and caught up with our mail and our friends.

On Monday we called in at Argentière to check the time of the earliest téléphérique, and I started to prepare for the next day. Tomorrow I had decided I would try and climb the Allain-Leininger route on the North Face of the Petit Dru.

My rucksac was packed. I became a little uneasy, it seemed far too heavy. For what was primarily a rock climb, I hoped to climb in my comfortable Asolo La Rage rock shoes, but to get to the start of the route involved an icy couloir and glacier approach. The long descent also involved crossing glaciers, so I would have to wear my Asolo plastic boots on the approach and then carry them on the rock climbing. The same went for my axes and crampons. The usual technique for climbs like the North Face of the Dru for a rope of two climbers is for the lead climber to climb encumbered whilst the second carries the rucksac. Unfortunately, by choosing to climb alone I would have to manage it all myself.

I was a little uneasy about three things: the approach, the climb and the descent. Which seemed pretty comprehensive for starters. But all were new to me. I had spent hours, time and time again studying photographs, descriptions and the map to try and memorise as much as I could. I went through the equipment I was going to carry, and discarded as much as possible; I even went to the extent of removing the alloy slats from the rucksac back support. To pare down weight even further, I cut out the descriptions and photographs from my guide books and separated them into three plastic sleeves – approach, route and descent. Then I cut the map down to the minimum size I would require to find the way from the Charpoua

Hut and folded that too into a plastic sleeve. Maybe none of this obsessive paring down achieved much, but psychologically I felt a lot better.

TUESDAY 17TH AUGUST

I woke around 5.30 a.m. and took a look outside. There was a lot of early morning cloud around, shrouding Les Vertes. What was happening to the weather?

Yet the météo forecast was good. By 6.00 a.m. it all started to look a bit better. I was feeling more positive with the arrival of the day and carried on with my breakfast.

At 6.20 a.m. I woke JB for a lift to Argentière and the Grands Montets. Loading the sleepy children into the back of Perkins, we chugged off and by 6.50 a.m. I was stood on the doorstep of the téléphérique station, awaiting the arrival of the workmen and the first cabin. By the time this had arrived so had an old friend from Lobuche and Kangtega, Marc Twight, an American currently living in Chamonix. He was up and about because he was keen to climb a route on the Aiguille Sans Nom.

We chatted on the téléphérique and walked across towards the descent couloir together. Finding it in horrid and unstable dry condition we abseiled down, then down-climbed the last part to a jumble of loose boulders perched precariously in the lower half. Negotiating a way down on to and across the Nant Blanc Glacier, we steamed across towards the base of the Aiguille Sans Nom, where I left Marc to go up, while I continued down the glacier and over the bergschrund to join the Drus glacier. I was now heading up to the base of the North Face at last.

It looked cold, grey and miserable. The hardest part seemed to be getting started. The ice extended a good distance from the rock, and there was a narrow ridge of ice connecting to it which continued up a rock slab a further ten or so metres, finally to peter out at a steep rocky corner. I was going to have to climb this first section in crampons; there was no way I could negotiate the ice in rock shoes and I would have to carry on up this very awkward-looking corner in boots as well. Sinking crampons and axes into the thin hard ice, I teetered on up and, reaching the top, and tucked my axe away. With a deep breath I tried to get some kind of handhold on the loose wet rock to climb my way through the little overhang and up the corner into a groove. It was loose with hard small pebbles of granite everywhere. I cleaned out the cracks before thrusting in my hands and fighting my way up. Cold, dirty and loose – I was keen to be up and off it as soon as possible. Forty metres up on a little ledge I came across my first team of climbers of the day. They were three Bulgarians, two lads and a lass, who had spent the night bivvied under the route and seemed to be less than pleased at my arrival. Even less so as I overtook them and, no matter how careful I was, could not avoid tiny rocks falling down the next loose couloir on top of them. It was loose and horrid, a mixture of old ice and part-frozen blocks, but not steep. I was soon up and out of it and, finding a suitable spot, at least was able to take off my rucksac, crampons and plastic boots and exchange them for a nice lightweight pair of rock shoes. The weight was now off my feet – but all on to my back!

I took out the route description and looked up. A series of slabs led to some loose blocks. I had forgotten about all the recent rockfalls from the Dru due to the drying-out of the mountain with a succession of dry summers. Above these the route heads up towards some cracks and chimney systems leading to a flake line rightwards. The cracks were not icy, but unfortunately they were still wet, and as I sank my arm happily into a monster jam, my smile turned into a grimace as I felt the water trickle its way through.

The rock was solid now and at last I was actually feeling secure, making a rising traverse right. I reached the point where the pillar joined the smooth wall above at an awkward crack. This looked to be what I can only describe as nasty! A solid flake of granite rose up parallel to the wall behind, leaving a crack that was just about big enough for me to squeeze inside and worm up. The problem would be my rucksac. With it on there was no way I would be able to chimney up and I was unsure of being able to hold on to it as I climbed.

I decided to get out the Cairngorm rope I had brought along for my abseil descent, fasten one end to myself, and the other to my sac. Then carefully placing this on the ledge leaning in to the rock, I coiled the rope on top so that it would feed out freely. Now, assuming the rucksac did not fall and pull me off, and/or vice versa, once at the top I would be able to find a secure spot and haul it up. So I was set. I climbed into the chimney, braced knees and elbows, and gradually wormed my way up. Battered and bruised, I was soon on the ledge above and clipping myself into an in situ belay peg and proceeded to drag the rucksac up after me, keeping it away from the chimney so as not to get it jammed at the slight narrowing near the top.

Rope coiled and rucksac back on, it was now time to traverse right using an exposed horizontal ledge to reach the base of the famous Fissure Lambert.

A positive crack led to a strenuous little roof and then easier angled rock led to couloir chimney. As I followed this system of cracks up to the lower extremity of the Niche, I soon caught up with two English lads, who had also been bivouacking at the foot of the face. I remained behind for a couple of pitches and chatted. Then as they started across the Niche I decided to take advantage of my extensive wardrobe and once again donned plastic boot outers and crampons and tip-toed my way rightwards to the edge of the snow- and icefield and the edge of the face below. Down to my right the rock dropped away steeply and impressively in sheer granite walls. Exhilarated, I tucked back left, continued up another pitch of ice-rock, removed crampons and boots, on with the rock shoes, and off up again through the couloir and rocks to the large terrace above.

It was time for a look at the route description once more. I studied the next few pitches carefully and weighed up exactly where to go. Shouting cheerio down to the English lads I traversed left into a chimney. On steeper but solid ground again I climbed the vertical chimney to reach a diedre which led to a platform on the left. Another crack again, and then a slight descent to the left to avoid a wider crack, and I was in a fine position directly overlooking the Niche. A vertical crack led to a smaller niche, below a steep wall. I stepped left and followed an awkward vague line of ledges. This took me to the base of a long steep crack in an open corner. It looked hard. It was the line taken by the first ascensionists, the famous Fissure Allain and in retrospect would have been the best and most direct line to take. However, nowadays most people avoid the Fissure Allain by taking a different line, discovered on the sixth ascent, and I decided to do likewise. Traversing right below the crack, I was soon into the Boîte aux Lettres (the Letter Box). Having got myself established in it, all I had to do was continue to pass through between this flake of rock and the rockwall, in order to descend the other side to make a step right and reach the steep slab starting up rightwards towards the challenge, the Fissure Martinetti. This all seemed very straightforward until I started to work my way down. The further I descended, the tighter it became. The walls enclosed me and my rucksac became wedged between them. As I wriggled to try to free myself, my feet parted company with the rock and I found myself momentarily suspended in space, rucksac jammed, but legs akimbo! Trying not to panic and half wanting to laugh at the seriousness of the situation, I gathered myself together and tried to work out the best solution. There was no way I could descend further and get out of the Boîte, as the further down I went the narrower it became and the more I would be jammed. I urgently needed to restore contact between my feet and the rock. Loosening my sac, I indulged in some violent thrashing and I was able to inch back up and get free. Now the way out would be to descend very airily facing into the rock-crack with my rucksac outside the crack. All very insecure, but at least I would not get jammed this time. Gritting my teeth I tried to jam elbows and knees across the crack and descend. The main problem was I was now unable to see where I was going and had to feel my way down with my feet. Another couple of metres further and I could make a wide straddle right and feel the relief and security of arriving at the bottom of the slab!

The next pitch was supposed to be fairly hard but, relieved to be out of the Boîte aux Lettres and with adrenalin now flowing well, so did I and was soon sitting at the top of the pitch smiling at the absurdity of my previous situation!

An awkward crack and then a steep and strenuous wall and I was on the third large platform overlooking the West Face. I took a moment to look down that formidable face. Another day, I promised myself. One should always have something for another day.

From here the climbing lay leftwards and up, still solid rock, but more broken, with cracks leading through and over little chimneys. I knew I was getting there. My arms feeling slightly the worse for wear, the adrenalin no longer flowing, as the early afternoon clouds rolled in I rolled on up. I met two Dutch lads who had climbed the West Face by the American Direct and then I was on the top. No views again. I had been granted a chance to climb, but not to relish any Alpine panoramas. I would have to return should I want to see more, I told myself, thinking of the West Face.

Time to go down. The Dutch lads were new to the mountain too, so we exchanged ideas on the topo of the descent and, again pooling ropes, set off on the long road down.

This weather had been a magnet. The first 'beaux temps' all summer. Everyone had pulled out the stops to climb a route and, as we descended, teams started to appear from off the Bonatti Pillar,

April in Chamonix!

Now and then Kate needed a cuddle. So did her mother.

Tom at school, ignoring the bolts.

Solo, centre picture, on the limestone seacliffs of the Calanques, above.

Training on granite at Col des Montets, below left.

Ice-climbing practice on the Mont Blanc Glacier, below right.

The first half of the Big Six: above left, the Grandes Jorasses; above right, the Matterhorn through the clouds; below the Eiger – taxing mountains with long and famous histories.

Boarding the train, Eiger-bound, above left.

A dizzy view down from the Lauper Face to the distant campsites and tourism of Kleine Scheidegg, above right.

Alison, a minute figure in the middle of a snow-plastered North Face, below.

Above left, the Badile, the North Face to the left, the North Ridge on the right-hand skyline.

Looking back at the Czech climbers whom Alison passed on the route, above right.

On the lower part of the North Ridge, as Alison descends from her successful solo, below.

The Drus, with the Grandes Jorasses behind, above.

Alison at the Niche, below left.

Climbers descending from the Flammes de Pierre, below right.

Alison, a speck on the 500-metre North Face of the Cima Grande, above left.

Alison and the children walking near the Tri Cima, above right.

The Tri Cima di Lavaredo, below.

Alison, the day after completing the Big Six, enjoying the Dolomites with Tom and Kate.

Swallows and Amazons for ever!

JB and the faithful Perkins at Perkins' personal high point in the Auronzo Hut car park.

including a very sorry-looking team from the US, Dan and Dave, miserable after two days on the route and a rucksac of vital bivvi gear dropped on the first day! Next we were joined by two French whippets who had slept at the Charpoua Hut and done the route in a day, climbing over all the other teams, and still just got back to the hut that night! After a sociably laidback descent I realised, on arriving at the col of the Flammes de Pierre, that I was myself cutting it a bit fine this late in the day with no bivvi gear. So I decided to put a spurt on. Leaving the Americans to pick up the gear they had left on their way up, and a hundred other pairs of climbers of all nationalities bivouacking before their ascent, I scooted on down the back side of the Flammes de Pierre to catch up with the French whippets just before darkness. A brief pause to clip on my crampons and headlamp, and then we watched each other as we negotiated the holes and descended the glacier together.

Before I knew it, the hut was looming in front of me at the bottom of the ridge. *Brilliant.* Time for a brew and a good night's sleep, but no, the guardienne had finished cooking, the hut was full to bursting. Everyone was already in bed and even the French whippets had had their beds taken over!

A friendly French guide offered me a can of Coke and I was presented with some blankets. 'There will be a place at 2.00 a.m.,' the guardienne assured me. So, with the promise of at least a half night's sleep I went down the slopes to lay my tired body on a flat terrace, a wee bit rocky, but with enough grassy bits for comfort lying on my rucksac lining mat and overtrousers. Using my rope as a pillow, I wrapped myself round with the blankets and slid into the huge thin plastic bivouac bag I had carried. At first it felt great. I was weary and it was wonderful to be horizontal, looking up at the stars and watching the tracks of satellites and aeroplanes. But bliss did not last, and as hunger and thirst set in, so did the cold. The ground started to feel hard and I could not sleep. I watched the hut door.

Around 1.40 a.m. I could hear voices in the hut; the first of the early risers were up. I'd nip in now and ensure I got a bed space. Alas, only two people had got up and there was still no room as it had been overful before. 'Come back in another hour,' the guardienne told me sharply. No chance, I thought, the hut was warm, there was no way I was going back out to reconstruct my bivouac in the cold. I found a tiny stool, sat down on it, put blankets over my shoulders and snuggled down! As I watched her prepare toast and coffee for the departing climbers I could not help myself drooling! My stomach rumbled harder than ever and my mouth was drying up in anticipation. Only five hours to breakfast, but what I really needed was sleep.

2.30 a.m. and more excitement, climbers crawled from their snuggly pits. As the gaps appeared I weighed up the best slot and without waiting to be called, crawled on to a soft mattress and covered myself with a wonderful soft quilt. As their toast sent delicious smells across the room, I drifted off into a deep sleep . . .

I woke around 6.00 a.m. – it was light and I was hungry. The morning was beautiful, clear as a bell, and the mountains stunning. I looked up at the rocky slopes of the Dru and thought of all the other teams up there enjoying themselves.

Finally the guardienne was up again, put the coffee on and started to set out places. I asked if there was enough for me too. A group of us sat around the table and demolished café au lait with lots of 'au lait' and toast piled high with ample quantities of jam and butter. There was no rush to get down. Plenty of time to chat and everyone wanted to do that. The delightful elegant French lady beside me asked if I too had walked up to the hut. 'No,' I replied, 'I have been climbing.' But where was my partner? 'No, I was on my own.' And what have you climbed? When I told them a respectful hush fell over the table.

They seemed impressed and requested to know what else I had solo climbed – suddenly everyone became interested! Though some people pretend it is not, climbing is hugely competitive, so I had been particularly cagey as to who I had hitherto told about my Big Six campaign. No point in laying your cards on the wrong table.

By now I felt I was well on the way to achieving my goal. Even if someone else now picked up the idea of doing a route solo on each of the six, they would have their work cut out to catch up with me. So I explained that whilst I was fairly sure none of my intended routes had previously had female solo ascents, the more I got into the project it became apparent that I might even be the first person to have tried a solo on each . . . the Dru certainly had had very few solo ascents and that narrowed the odds considerably.

Now well on target, I was happy to discuss the climbs openly and my future intentions. Everyone was incredibly encouraging and I was sworn to promise I would write a book by the delightful French lady, who proceeded to finish her make-up and return to Montenvers. It was all a touch overwhelming.

I could not help wondering if speaking out the night before might not have earned me a full night's sleep and something to eat and drink!

It was time to go down. A delightful new path had been carved out of the grassy slopes down to the Mer de Glace. I went down with Dan and Dave. We picked flowers to press for Dan's girlfriend and drank at the refreshing, sparkling streams.

At Montenvers Station we parted, the lads to ride to Chamonix by train, me to set off for my long pleasant walk to Les Bois.

JB: A real clear morning. Well, she should be on her way down, or at least moving from a very cold bivouac. We get on with breakfast and suddenly notice all the campsite with binoculars trained on the Dru. One, two, three helicopters in action working across the summit. Is it a major rescue? I ignore it, as do the children, and find out later that it was the filming of a commercial.

Alison strolls into town looking cool and chuffed. Perhaps she would like a brew?

The Comici route on the North Face of
Cima Grande (2999m)

11

CIMA GRANDE DI LAVAREDO – 2999m

I wish some day to make a route and from the
summit let fall a drop of water and this is where my
route will have gone.

Emilio Comici

The Dolomites are like no other part of the Alps and I was
looking forward to an entirely new experience. The first thing you
have to do is avoid having mountain double vision because most
of the peaks go under two names, depending on whether you are
taking a German or an Italian view of this border region. The
central area of the Tre Cime di Laveredo (Drei Zinnen) is now a
national park with lots of huts and a network of waymarked paths
which make exploring very easy. It is difficult today to imagine
how this magical area could have been such a brutal battlefield in
the First World War.

The Cima Grande (Grosse Zinne) at 2999 metres is the highest
summit in a famous trinity with, looking north, the slender spire of
Punta Frida, the Cima Piccola and the Cima Piccolissima to its left
and the squatter Cima Ovest to its right. Just to increase the confusion
there are actually six summits in the group, not three, and that's
nothing to do with mountain pseudonyms. The Cima Grande was first
ascended from the gentler southern side which lurks above the main
path in from the Auronzo Hut. This is the route that the descent is
now based on.

The North Face is 500 metres high and the bottom half flat and rather featureless. The only real natural line is a prominent corner system cutting down the top half of the face from the summit. At the foot of the face, almost below this, is a tiny pillar of less than good rock leaning against the wall. It was a start, and all the climber with vision required was the ability to link them together. But would he be a German or an Italian? National rivalry was intense and fuelled by the press at each attempt.

Leading contender among the Italians was the enigmatic Emilio Comici, a big-wall specialist who articulated the perfect definition of a diretissima route with the quote at the beginning of this chapter. By the summer of 1933 he had got higher than any of his rivals and left a white handkerchief on the face to mark the spot he had achieved the previous year.

On 13th August he roped up with the Dimai brothers, Angelo and Giuseppe. This time success was theirs!

The lower 250-metre wall was steeper than they expected. When measured it was found to overhang the base by over twenty metres. They placed seventy-five pitons to overcome this section, bivouacked on the face and climbed the more reasonable upper corner system to the summit next day. There were of course critics of the number of pitons used. But, as usual with these mighty north faces, they voiced their criticism from their armchairs at home.

The second ascent of the route was also made by Comici when he climbed it solo the following year in a remarkable three and a half hours.

Time has in the end judged Comici's climb on the North Face well. It has not only become established as one of the magical Big Six but it is sought after by climbers from all over the world as a great rock climb on a great face. And for those with enough skill it can today be climbed free.

The way Comici wrote about climbing still finds a responsive echo with today's climbers.

The climber who is able to divine the most logical and the most elegant way of reaching a summit, disdaining the easy slopes, and then follows that way, his nerves stretched to the limit, sensing his own inner conflict and aware of the effort needed to overcome the drag of the depths at his heels and the swirl of space around him, that climber is creating a true work of art, sometimes of exceptional quality. A product of the spirit, an aesthetic sense of man which will last for ever carved on the rock walls, as long as the mountains themselves have life.

This certainly applies to his own solo climb.

Now it was my turn to visit the mighty rock towers which rose so magnificently out of the pleasant pastures below. It was almost sixty years to the day since the first ascent by Comici, fifty years since the first female ascent of the face, and now I wanted to try and solo the classic route on the central of the Tre Cima – the Grande.

In my early years of climbing, limestone had been my favourite medium. I had spent many evenings and Sundays with my best schoolmate, Bev England, relishing the delightful finger-pocketed dolomitic limestone of Harborough and Brassington Rocks, the steeper faces of Cromford's Willersley and Wildcat crags and the fame of Stoney Middleton. Its general steepness didn't bother me, as its formation usually made for a variety of cracks and ledges offering a sequence of holds and I enjoyed the intricacy of the climbing.

I recognised of course that the Dolomites were in a different league of things and I remembered Spike's friendly warning. He had climbed in the area some years before and suggested I put off taking a walk around the base of the great faces until I was ready to climb them. 'Just don't go round and look up,' he advised.

Apart from some bouldering on Harborough, I had given limestone very little attention over recent years, but I still felt happy about the climbing, although maybe just a little concerned at my overall rock fitness.

After a big route I usually like a few days to unwind and play with the children. But my time was running out. It was now 20th August and I had to be in Munich by the beginning of September. Before that we had to get to the Dolomites and I had to climb the last of my Big Six. I now had some extra pressure to cope with. It had become apparent that if I could climb the Comici route on the Cima Grande in under four hours my total climbing time for the Six would be under twenty-four hours. It was a tempting goal to aim for.

So we chugged our way steadily through Switzerland and, after a peaceful night in Perkins on the edge of Bern, we carried on our journey into Austria, over the Brenner Pass and headed south to the quiet corner of northern Italy. Not far now. Arriving at the edge of Misurina we stopped to let Perkins' radiator cool down, as we still had a very steep toll road to climb up to the Auronzo Hut which is where you park for the Tre Cime.

We drove on and up. The road was steep and got steeper. High above us I caught a glimpse of the sun shining on the glass windows of a building. But that was way higher than we were going, surely? Or was it? The zig-zags increased. Would Perkins make it? Even in his lowest gear ratio the engine temperature gauge had long gone off the scale. I was silent, even Tom and Kate went quiet, absorbed in the struggle. For two solid days Perkins had given his best, chugging us merrily across Europe, now he was being tested to the limit.

Around 8.00 p.m. we arrived and crept slowly on to the vast car parking terraces beneath the Auronzo Hut, following signs to the 'camper van' level.

At 2300 metres the air was light and fresh. There were wispy clouds blowing around. But as the sun set the lofty rocky mountaintops showed themselves and the views were ethereal. It was a delight to be there. We went to sleep to the distant tinkle of cow bells.

We were based on the south side of the Tre Cime so next morning set out on a contouring walk east which would take us up to the Forcella Lavaredo from where we would be able to see what we had come for, the famous north faces.

The weather was misty and cloudy, but with odd breaks as the sun shone through to reveal some magical views. Great rock peaks and towers soared dramatically out of grassy Alpine pastures. The Dolomites were even more beautiful than I had imagined. We contoured slowly round past the Auronzo Hut and crept quietly past the Alpini Chapel as the many tourists were engrossed in a Sunday service. At the Lavaredo Hut we set down our rucksacs amongst the boulders and grass to have a snack and watch the Sunday rock climbers on the South-east faces. Then it was time to move. The air was thinner now but we strode on up the hill to the Forcella Lavaredo, the col at the east end of the Tre Cime. From here I had my first chance to view the famous North Face of the Cima Grande and Cima Ovest.

Here was the last of my Big Six. And it was big and steep! Had I not climbed the five, had I not prepared mentally to climb this one, I think I would have walked away and said no!

My experience of Dolomite walls was nil. My rock climbing level these past few months not very high, and here was one of the most impressive classic rock walls in the Alps. I reasoned with myself that I had come all this way to climb this wall and now I had at least to give it a shot.

But I needed another twenty-four hours to recover from two days cooped up in Perkins, not to mention all the strenuous cracks and chimneys of the Petit Dru. So next day I climbed the via ferrata that links the Forcella Lavaredo with the Locatelli Hut. Originally constructed as part of Italy's First World War defences, some of these airy iron ladder and tunnel ways look as if they haven't been serviced since, with their rubble-strewn ledges and rusty wire hawsers. But after climbing a small peak behind the Locatelli Hut, I felt a lot fitter. I was ticking over well and had had another appetite-whetting view of the Tre Cime.

TUESDAY 24TH AUGUST

I awoke around 5.30 a.m. to a cloudy morning. We had had some rain in the night and it had been windy. I felt unsure about the weather but, after watching the clouds, got up anyway around 7.30 a.m. and climbed out of Perkins to sit quietly and eat my breakfast. Although there was a red sky, which in England I knew to be a bad sign, things started to look a lot more promising. Eight-thirty a.m. and it was time to go.

At the Forcella Lavaredo I started to gear up, harness fastened, hardware clipped in, my Cairngorm 9 mm rope tied up Alpine-style on my back, chalk bag fastened, Cassin helmet on. I topped up with Isostar and Jordan's Frusli and tucking some spares with gloves and headband into my waist bag, I tied up my rucksac, tucked it under a boulder and set off.

As I left the col three other climbers appeared. I was concerned that they might be going on to the Comici as well. I did not really want them directly behind me, on my tail. But on the other hand, a team of three would be so much slower that it was not a good idea to follow them! I chewed over the problem as I continued to contour across to the base of the Grande. Happily, when I stopped at the foot of the pillar which is the start of the climb, they continued on past me and headed towards another route on the Cima Ovest.

Relieved, I unfastened my harness and had what was to be my last toilet stop of the climb Then I took off my windbreak and tucked it into my waist bag. The face was sheltered from the wind and it was going to be warm work. I was ready, it was time to start. We had lost our Alpine Club Guide Book the day before, but fortunately JB had managed to borrow a German one from two friendly Berlin climbers at the car park, and we had made a trace of the relevant page which I studied one more time, before tucking it away and getting to work.

The first eighty metres was a loose scramble leading up the side of the pillar that leans against the base of the face. A steep crack led to another ledge at the start of the hard climbing. I found the crack committing, but carried on climbing to reach the start of the hard pitches. The steepness of the wall became apparent but another thirty metres of climbing had been gained.

The first crux pitch looked hard and it seemed to have a few key pitons missing, if my topo was to be believed. I climbed a few more moves to where the pitch moved left. That looked hard, too. I climbed down for a short rest, then up again. The moves left still looked hard. I was waiting for the energy to flow from within.

I went back down to the ledge to think. I decided I could safely trail my rope as the rock was so sheer. I would have more freedom of movement and, keeping the rope end clipped through my Soloist, I would be ready and prepared should I decide on any pitches I wanted to back-rope myself.

I was having slight doubts as to the whole climb. What if other pitches had been depegged too? I was relying on clipping into odd pegs for my protection. I became a little anxious.

It had taken a while to get going, but this time, as I started up again, I knew that although I was not yet climbing smoothly or well, I would keep going.

The pressure was on. I was climbing slowly. The clock was ticking away. If I carried on as slowly as this I would not achieve my goal. There was a lot of hard rock climbing to come. I clipped in at the belay stance and once more studied my topo.

The next two pitches passed quickly in a blur of concentration. So now I had done three. What next? A large groove-corner system, with a crack in the back, it looked hard, but it went well. The holds were positive and I was strong. At last the flow was starting to come back. With every move the climbing became easier, not the rock, but me. It was supposed to be awkward and I was having a ball. The pitches went more quickly and I felt as if things were finally taking a turn for the better. I felt in control of the situation and no longer worried by the

112

number of hard pitches. Take your time, pace yourself and just enjoy climbing with care, I told myself.

JB: The children and I had a slow breakfast. I had arranged to pick up Alison's rucksac from the side of the path from the col down to the face. Kate wanted to walk as well as Tom. However her little legs soon tired and I hoisted her on to my shoulders. Tom strolled on using a lightweight Cassin axe as a walking stick. The weather looked okay and soon we were at the col. The children wanted to know where Mum was climbing. I pointed vaguely to the North Face of the Cima Grande. Fine. They wanted to build walls. I wanted to take photographs and get out the binoculars. Leaving the children squabbling about sharing out the stones, I ran down the col and soon spotted Alison's rucksac. Now out with the binoculars. She did look tiny but, as ever, was moving steadily up the hard climbing. We went back to building drystone walls.

I was in control now and I could feel happy again. I knew I was climbing well. My confidence restored I started to move more quickly, and unhampered, and was soon climbing my way through the last steep pitches towards the bivouac site where the angle eased off. As I rested on yet another small ledge I remembered the purple passages in Gaston Rébuffat's *Starlight and Storm* 'only one ledge, tiny at that to rest on . . .'

Before I knew it, I was there, a spacious yet sloping bivouac spot. Now the angle eased back past vertical. The climbing would get easier and my speed increase, or would it? The hard and steep bottom half had taken just under two and a half hours. Now it was time to motor.

JB: I watched from time to time and wandered off taking telephoto shots. The children played on and Tom found some old wood for the roof beams of his house. The wind started to increase and clouds were gathering. We ate an early lunch. It was starting to get chilly on the col. Alison had particularly asked me not to take the children down under the face for two reasons. Firstly, sound rises and she did not want the noise of the children at play to distract her and secondly she was a little concerned about the loose stones near the top of the face falling on anyone below. I decided to pack the two rucksacs into one and slowly move down to watch her on the descent on the opposite side of the mountain. The last sight of Alison going upwards was as she shot at speed from the bivouac ledge system to be hidden by the big upper corner.

A swig of Isostar, a study of the topo and on up into the huge roof and corner system above.

I traversed left into the back of the upper corner system and romped my way up the back of the corner. A second corner arrived. I stepped left to a wet and greasy chimney and then right into another corner, but with less rock this time. No sign of any pitons! The higher I climbed the looser it became and then wetter. It was raining, the clouds were down and water was dripping from the back wall.

This led into a horrible cave-like niche with a huge roof on the left and a wide dripping overhanging crack above that looked slimy and unlikely.

JB: As we walked down from the col to the Lavaredo Hut it started to rain and the clouds came down even further. Tom asked about the rain and Mum and I feigned indifference. Tom and Kate had a boulder by the hut and then it started to rain properly. The tourists were scattering, we put on our waterproofs.

I felt I had climbed into a blind alley. Still I had faith in my route-finding ability. Somewhere here had to be the start of the long traverse left and then only two pitches before the Ringband, the distinctive traverse line at the end of the hard climbing and a couple of pitches below the top. I had followed the topo exactly, so surely I had to be correct. But did the route traverse above the roof or below it, maybe I had climbed too high and I should traverse beneath it?

I teetered left on to a rock nose and looked down and across. The rock was orange, bright and loose. I could see odd rope slings and pegs dotted about in various places, but it did not feel right. No. Where I was had to be the way. Although I had lost the line of the traverse, at least the rock was solid above the roof to climb across. So the decision was made. I would traverse above the roof, or if that attempt failed, at least I could continue up the wet and slimy groove-chimney system that I was in.

It was raining hard. I tried to clean the smooth soles of my Asolo La

Rage rock boots on my trousers one more time, then started to climb up into the dripping groove-chimney above. I made a move and I was committed, but I was relieved. Not only could I see some slimy chalk marks at the edge of the chimney, but also above me, deep into the crack, was a peg. A fine shiny peg in a stream of water, just waiting for me to spot it. I climbed on up, soon over the little roof and out of the chimney and on to the edge of the traverse.

The topo gave the traverse as a pitch of IV+/AD, so I assumed there would be plenty of pegs to follow. But no, again no pegs to be seen. Maybe it went higher. I had made my decision, it looked fine exactly where I was; pegs or not, it did not matter to me. Whilst it would be a spacey traverse moving left directly above the lip of the huge roof, it felt no more committing than the steep pitches below. It was now raining heavily. I was not going to hang around.

The upper corner system is not as steep as the lower wall and I was concerned that my trailing rope might snag. As I arrived at each ledge I had been pulling up my Cairngorm 9 mm rope, re-coiling it and laying it carefully so that my end was at the top. Setting out up the chimney I had done the same. My fear now was that as I climbed to the end of the traverse, and the arc of the weight of the rope between me and the ledge increased, it would pull all the coiled rope off the ledge and swing into space, giving me a hefty tug as it did so. Anxious not to have the worry, I pulled the rope up and stacked it behind a spike at the start of the traverse line and set off.

As soon as I moved sideways my confidence was once more restored and of course the first hidden piton revealed itself and yet again I knew I was on the correct line.

The climbing was great! Not at all hard, just spacey and I relished my splendid isolation at the end of the traverse. Quickly pulling in the rope, I re-coiled it Alpine-style around me and set off to finish the last two delightful pitches to reach the famous Ringband. In the past climbers have carried on up the loose rock and gully pitches from here to the summit, but nowadays most parties finish here at the end of the best climbing, for a traverse to the South Face and descent.

I glanced at my Rolex, and felt a warm glow of relief. This top half, although it had felt slow, had taken under an hour. So I had climbed the whole route in under three and a half hours. Now I could relax. The pressure was off. I had reached my goal. The trick was to be careful and to get down safely.

I had arrived at the Ringband just before 2.00 p.m. in rain, cloud and gusting wind. Great! Now for the way off. This was obvious. A level bedding plane led right into the mist, well trodden and, even in this light, easy to follow, like a narrow ledge between a metre and fifty centimetres wide, as if someone had taken an enormous chisel and carved a ledge right round the mountain some fifty metres below the top. Cautiously, I started to walk along it. A slip here would mean a 500-metre fall. At one point I came across a part where it was very low under a roof, and the ledge had collapsed, so that I had to get on hands and knees. Spilt chalk showed that so had everyone else. I crawled across the gap underneath the roof.

Back on my two feet, I soon came to the most western point of the Ringband and the North-west Ridge and could make a sharp left turn on to the gentler South Face. Immediately a cold wind hit me. I took a quick look at the copied topo. 'Follow the Ringband into the centre of the South Face, until under the very summit.' Perhaps it would have helped if I could have seen one hand in front of the other. It was of course still raining, maybe harder now! Passing some fine well-used bivvi sites I found a cairn marking the start of the descent route. There was a bolt in situ and fixed rope, but it looked quicker to down-climb awhile, down the middle gully system with its red and blue paint markings to a very polished and in these conditions very slippery chimney. This is the crux pitch of the Grohmann-Innerkofler South Face climb and is graded III. Off my back came my fifty metres of Cairngorm 9 mm rope and I abseiled down. Two more short abseils and more cairns and red paint led me down to the scree-covered ledges that cut across the South Face at one-third height.

The most well-marked way seemed to head left (as I faced into the mountain) on a horizontal traverse line. Soon I lost the cairns and paint, but not the line. At the base of a steep wall with almost no visibility I found an anchor. I abseiled down, traversed left on loose ground to a huge looming flake with in situ slings and abseiled again. Then a down-climb to the top of a short chimney system brought me at last to the screes below. My fear on the descent had been of lightning. I had heard the stories of Dolomite electric storms, and they had spurred my descent of the South Face. But the mountain had been kind. It had let another solitary survive its rocky face and, although stirring with discontent, had not dislodged me in anger.

JB: We walked down towards Perkins, sheltering to have a drink under the eaves of the Alpi Chapel. The South Face was covered with clouds and if anything it was raining harder. Whilst the children drank, I scanned the clouds. In a short wind-blown break I was sure there was a little figure just crossing the Ringband after coming round the North-west Ridge. It should be Alison, but was I imagining the sighting? The clouds closed in again. A helpful sheltering Italian said it was 2.10 p.m. We carried on back to Perkins.

My head was nicely dry under my Cassin helmet, but my legs and feet were soaked. It was chucking it down. I was off the screes and back on the main track. Sodden tourists were fleeing in various directions. I sprinted down the road in a torrential downpour and, as he saw me from Perkins, I gave JB a thumbs-up – two thumbs and four fingers. I had done my Big Six, and in a total climbing time of twenty-three and three-quarter hours.

It had been a hard day's summer.

APPENDICES

Twinkle, twinkle little star
How I wonder what you are
Up above the world so high

Anon/Traditional

I

A CLIMBING DIARY
26/3/93–10/11/93

OUTCROPS AND BOULDERS
numerous visits throughout the period

Les Houches	Chamonix – Mont Blanc
La Joux	
Le Fayet/La Panthère Rose	
Les Gaillands	
Servoz	
Col de Sormiou	Calanques
Dalle de Port Miou	
Blocs du Casset	Cerces
Puy Maubert	
Cerces-Bez	
Ailefroide Secteur Dalles	Les Ecrins
Fissure d'Ailefroide	
Tête de la Druye	
Fissure d'Aile	
Blocs du Col des Montets	Chamonix-Mont Blanc
Mur Avalanche	
L'Aiguillette d'Argentière	
Les Cheserys	
Vallorcine	
Chennavoir	
Dalle d'Arveyron	
Pierre d'Orthaz	

ROCK CLIMBS

11.4.93	Voie Saphir	D–	Calanques-En Vau
12.4.93	Voie de la Sans Nom	AD	
12.4.93	Voie de la Passarelle	D+	
12.4.93	Cheminée Castelveil	PD	
13.4.93	Arête des Huit Gendarmes	AD	Calanques-Vallon des Rampes
13.4.93	Arête de la Flèche	AD	
14.4.93	Sirène Liautard	D–	Calanques-En Vau

15.4.93	Arête Intégrale du Cloportes	AD	Calanques-Vallon des Rampes
15.4.93	Voie des Ronces	AD+	
16.4.93	Voie de la Calanque	D	Calanques-En Vau
16.4.93	Grande Aiguille-Paillon	AD–	
16.4.93	Voie de Pouce Normale	AD+	
17.4.93	Traverse E-W	D–	Calanques-Les Lames
17.4.93	Arête S.E.	PD	Calanques-Rocher des Goudes
17.4.93	Semaphore (SW)	PD	
17.4.93	Arête de la Cordée	D+	Calanques-Rocher St Michel
18.4.93	Tour de la . . .	PD	Calanques-Bec de Sormiou
18.4.93	Arête de L'Extrême Bec	AD+	
19.4.93	Voie des Boudrières	D+	Calanques-Morgiou du Renard
20.4.93	Arête Sud	AD–	Calanques-Aiguille de Sugiton
20.4.93	Arête Nord	AD–	
20.4.93	Arête du Belvedere	AD	Calanques-Crête de St Michel
24.4.93	Eperon Ouest	D	Calanques-L'Eissadon
28.4.93	Super Sirène	D+	En Vau
29.4.93	Grande Arête de Marseille	D	Calanques-Candelle
29.4.93	Arête de Cassis	PD	
5.5.93	Arête de la Bruyère	AD	Cerces
12.5.93	Aiguillette Lauzet Couloir Sud	PD+	
15.5.93	Crête de Roche Bernard	PD	
27.5.93	Palavar Les Flots	D+	Les Ecrins
22.6.93	S.S.E. Face Aiguille de la Glière	D	Chamonix-Mont Blanc
1.8.93	Aiguille de la Persévérence, Arête Sud	AD+	
1.8.93	Aiguille de la Persévérence, Arête Ouest	AD	
1.8.93	Aiguille des Chamois, Arête Est	PD	
2.8.93	Aiguille de l'Index, Arête Sud-est	AD	

ALPINE CLIMBS

17.5.93	Pic des Près les Fonts: Couloir Davin	AD
24.5.93	Barre des Ecrins: Whymper Couloir/ Voie Normale	PD+
17.6.93	Grandes Jorasses: Shroud	TD+
29.6.93	Matterhorn: Schmid	TD+
8.7.93	Mönch: N.W. Spur, Nollen	D
9.7.93	Jungfrau: Voie Normale	PD+
24.7.93	Eiger: New Route	TD+
10.8.93	Piz Badile: Cassin	TD
17.8.93	Dru: Allain	TD
24.8.93	Cima Grande: Comici	ED–
29.10.93	Col du Plan: Lagarde Couloir	D+
10.11.93	Grandes Jorasses: Croz Spur	ED

ALL CLIMBS LISTED WERE SOLO ASCENTS

A KEY TO GRADES

PD	peu difficile – moderately difficult
AD	assez difficile – fairly difficult
D	difficile – difficult
TD	très difficile – very difficult
ED	extrêmement difficile – extremely difficult

II

A MOUNTAIN CHRONOLOGY

THE GRANDES JORASSES (4208m)

1865 The first ascent of the mountain to Pointe Whymper (4184m). Edward Whymper with Michel Croz, Christian Almer and Franz Biener.

1868 The first ascent of the highest summit, Pointe Walker (4208m). Horace Walker with Johann Juan, Julien Grange and Melchoir Anderegg.

1891 The first winter ascent, of Pointe Walker. Paulo Güssfeldt with Emile Rey, David Proment and Laurent and Fabien Croux.

1898 The first ascents of Pointes Marguerite (4065m) and Hélène (4054m). Apparently named after the ladies of the Duke of the Abruzzi who made the ascents with Laurent Croux, Joseph Petigax and Felix Ollier.

1904 The first ascent of Pointe Young (3996m). V.J.E. Ryan with Franz and Joseph Lochmatter.

1909 The probable first ascent of Pointe Croz (4101m). Frau E. Noll-Hasenclever with F. König, W. Klemm and R. Weitzenbach.

1911 The first descent of the Hirondelles Ridge. Geoffrey Winthrop Young and H. Owen Jones with Joseph Knubel and Laurent Croux.

1927 The first ascent of the Hirondelles Ridge. Sergio Matteoda and Francesco Ravelli, Gustavo Gaja, Guido Rivetti with Adolphe Rey and Alphonse Chenoz. The ascent was doubted until the second ascent by Pierre Allain and team in 1935 who found Rey's pitons in situ.

1931 The first attempts on the massive North Face. The main contenders were German and included Anderl Heckmair and Gustav Kröner, Franz and Toni Schmid, Willo Welzenbach and Ludwig Steinauer. Leo Brehm and Hans Rittler fell to their deaths. These attempts were based on and around the Central Icefield and its gully lines.

1932 The North Face was on every leading climber's shopping list. The prominent Walker and Croz Spurs were the fashion this season. Italian contenders included Boccalatte, Chabod, Carrel, Cretier, Benedetti, Binel, Maquignaz, Gervasutti and Zanetti. The French joined in with Armand Charlet and Robert Gréloz.

1935 The first ascent of the North Face via the Croz Spur by Rudolf Peters and Martin Meier. A fine reward for Rudolf Peters after his epic solo retreat in 1934 when his partner Peter Haringer was killed high on the spur in a fierce storm.

The second ascent and first by a woman. Guisto Gervasutti and Chabod roped up with Raymond Lambert and Loulou Boulaz because of terrible conditions and storms.

1938 The first ascent of the Walker Spur. Riccardo Cassin, Ugo Tizzoni and Gino Esposito. A fine stylish climb from the Italian master.

1948 The first winter ascent of the Hirondelles Ridge. Toni Gobbi and François Thomasset. A much underrated climb, considering the equipment and clothing available at that time.

1958 The first ascent of the Pointe Marguerite Spur. René Desmaison and Jean Couzy. René Desmaison's first new climb on the Grandes Jorasses, the first of many by this talented French maverick.

The first ascent of the Pointe Young Spur. Enrico Cavalieri and Andrea Mellano.

1964 The first winter ascent of the North Face and the Walker Spur. Walter Bonatti and Cosimo Zappelli.

1964 The first ascent of the Pointe Whymper Buttress. Walter Bonatti and Michel Vaucher in five storm-lashed days, with their ropes cut to bits.

1968 The first and winter ascent of the Shroud. René Desmaison and Robert Flematty. A much sought after last great Mont Blanc area problem.

The first solo ascent of the North Face and Walker Spur. Alessandro Gogna.

1970 The first ascent of the Pointe Hélène Spur by the Poles Woiciech Wröz, Eugeniusz Chrobak and Jacek Poreka.

1971 The first winter ascent of the Croz Spur. Georges Nominé and Claude Marmier.

1972 The first and winter ascent of the Central Icefield and Upper Right-Hand Gullies. The Japanese Yasuo Kanda, Yashuo Kato, Hideo Miyazuki, Toro Nakano and Kusuhide Saito. A long siege and many fixed ropes. However the whole route may not yet have had a second ascent (1993).

The first solo ascent of the Croz Spur. Jean Afanassief.

1973 The first and winter ascent of the East Flank of the Walker Spur. René Desmaison, Giorgio Bertone and Michel Claret. This side of the Walker Spur has not yet proved popular.

1974 The first solo ascent of the Shroud and in winter. Ivano Ghirardini.

1975 The first ascent of the Croz Direct. Helmut Kiene and Klaus Werner.

1976 The first ascent of the Central Icefield and Upper Left-Hand Gullies. Alex MacIntyre and Nick Colton. Alpine and splendid style from the British at last.

1977 The first winter ascent of Pointe Whymper by the Bonatti/Vaucher route. Pierre Béghin and Xavier Farglas. A much underrated ascent.

1978 The first winter solo ascent of the Croz Spur. Ivano Ghirardini.

1979 The first winter solo ascent of the Walker Spur. Tuneo Hasagaura.

1986 The first ascent of steep rock to the left of the Walker Spur. Patrick Gabarrou and Hervé Bouvard. A surprisingly good climb.

1990 The first solo ascent of Pointe Whymper by the Bonatti/Vaucher route. Slavko Sveticic. A very impressive performance.

1991 The first solo ascent of Pointe Young. Ivano Ghirardini.

1992 The first ascent and solo of the rock flank to the right of the Walker Spur. Marc Batard.

1993 The first ascent of the Central Icefield and Right-Hand Gullies to reach Pointe Whymper. Patrick Gabarrou et al.

THE MATTERHORN (4478m)

1857 The first oblique attempt which actually climbed the Tête du Lion. Abbé Gorrett with Jean-Jacques and Jean-Antoine Carrel.

1862 The first ascent of the mountain's south-west subsidiary summit, Pic Tyndall. Vaughan Hawkins, Samuel, Alfred and Charles Parker, Professor Tyndall with Joseph Bennen.

1865 The first ascent of the mountain by the Hörnli Ridge and the start of the legend. Edward Whymper, Charles Hudson, Douglas Hadow, Lord Francis Douglas with Michel Croz, Peter Taugwalder Snr and Peter Taugwalder Jnr. With the exception of Whymper and the Taugwalders, the rest of the party was killed in a fall on the descent. 'The day the rope broke.'

The first ascent of the Italian Ridge. Abbé Gorrett with Jean-Antoine Carrel, Jean-Baptiste Bich and Jean-Augustin Meynet.

1871 The first ascent by a woman. Lucy Walker, with guides.

1876 The first guideless ascent which earned the English climbers concerned, Colgrove, Cush and Cawood, a rebuke from *The Times*.

1879 The first ascent of the Zmutt Ridge. Alfred Mummery with Alexander Burgener, Johann Petrus and Augustin Gentinetta.

1882 The first winter ascent. Vittorio Sella with Jean-Antoine Carrel and Louis Carrel. A fine climb, up the Italian Ridge and down the Hörnli.

1898 The first solo ascent of the mountain by the Hörnli Ridge. Wilhelm Paulcke.

1911 The first ascent of the Furggen Ridge. Mario Piacenza with Jean-Joseph Carrel and Giuseppe Gaspard.

1931 The first ascent of the North Face. Franz and Toni Schmid. They were so poor they cycled from their Munich home to Zermatt.

1936 The first solo winter ascent of the mountain by the Italian Ridge. Giusto Gervasutti.

1944 The first female ascent of the Furggen Ridge. Loulou Boulaz et al.

1948 The first winter ascent of the Zmutt Ridge. Henri Masson with Edmund Petrig.

1952 The first winter ascent of the Furggen Ridge. Walter Bonatti and Roberto Bignami.

1959 The first solo ascent of the North Face. Dieter Marchardt.

1962 The first winter ascent of the North Face. Hilti Von Allmen and Paul Etter, Leo Schlommer and Erik Krempke, Werner Bittner, Peter Siegert and Rainer Kauschke. Amongst much TV and media attention!

1963 The first woman's ascent of the North Face. Michel Vaucher, Yvette Vaucher and Michel Darbellay.

1965 The first solo, winter ascent of the North Face via a new route. Walter Bonatti, in bad weather and closely followed by *Paris Match*.

1969 The first ascent of the Zmutt Nose, the rocky area between the Bonatti route on the North Face and the Zmutt Ridge. Leo Cerruti and Alessandro Gogna.

1972 A new route on the North Face, really a right-hand start to the Schmid route. V. Prokes, B.K. Adleik, L. Horka and Z. Drlik.

1974 The first winter ascent of the Zmutt Nose. Thomas Gross and Edgar Oberson.

1981 The first ascent of the Zmutt Nose Direct. Michel Piola and Pierre Allain Steiner.

1983 The first winter ascent of the Zmutt Nose Direct. Jan Wolf and Krzysztof Kraska.

1989 The first ascent of the Zmutt Nose Super Direct! Patrick Gabarrou and François Marsigny.

THE EIGER (3970m)

1858 The first ascent of the mountain by the South-West Flank. Charles Barrington with Christian Almer and Peter Bohren. Barrington had a fine way with words that would not have won any awards from the Swiss Tourist Board: 'They doubted if we had been on the top until a telescope disclosed the flag there. Thus ended my first and only visit to Switzerland. Not having enough money to try the Matterhorn, I went home.' He was Irish and a keen horseman.

1864 The first ascent of the mountain by a woman, by the South-West Flank. Lucy Walker et al.

1867 The first ascent of the South Ridge. G.E. Foster with Hans Baumann and Ulrich Almer.

1912 The famous railway through the Eiger commenced construction.

1921 The first ascent of the Mittellegi Ridge. Yuko Maki with Fritz Amatter, Fritz Steuri and Samuel Brawand.

1924 Mittellegi Hut built. Paid for by Yuko Maki.

1926 Fixed ropes placed on the Mittellegi Ridge to make it easier to guide clients. Perhaps it is time they were now removed!

1932 The first ascent of the North Face. The Lauper route. Hans Lauper, Alfred Zürcher with A. Graven and J. Knubel. 'A masterpiece of traditional climbing in the free style, mainly on ice but with at least one hard technical rock pitch. One of the finest routes of its class in the Alps,' wrote Robin Collomb.

1935 First attempt on the Eiger Nordwand. Max Sedlmayer and Karl Mehringer.

1937 First attempt of the South-East Face. O. Eidenschink and E. Moller.

Edi Rainer, Willy Angerer, Andreas Hinterstoisser and Toni Kurz pioneered what was to become the classic Nordwand route, but during the retreat in bad weather, tragically, they were all killed.

1938 First ascent of the Nordwand. The ultimate classic natural climbing line. Heinrich Harrer, Fritz Kasparek, Anderl Heckmair and Ludwig Vörg. This remarkable team was rapidly hijacked by the Nazi Party public relations team and eventually paraded with Adolf Hitler.

1961 First winter ascent of the North Face and 1938 route. Toni Hiebeler, Anton Kinshofer, Andreas Mannhardt and Walter Almberger. Planned and executed with considerable care and talent.

1963 First solo ascent of the North Face and 1938 route. Michel Darbellay. The great solo climber Walter Bonatti descended from his attempt as Darbellay started his.

First *descent* of the North Face. Paul Etter, Uli Ganterbein and Sepp Henkel.

1964 First woman's ascent of 1938 route. Daisy Voog and Werner Bittner.

First winter ascent of the Lauper. Hans Peter Trachsel and G. Siedof.

1966 First ascent of the Harlin Direct. Dougal Haston, Sigi Hupfauer, Jörg Lehne, Günther Strobel and Roland Votteler. A media-covered event, using fixed ropes and more climbers in supporting roles. The American John Harlin was killed during the final push when a fixed rope broke.

1968 First ascent of the North Pillar. The Polish climbers K. Cielecki, T. Lankytys, R. Szarferski and A. Zyzak climbed a wandering line that started well to the right of the North Pillar and eventually wound its way to finish up the Lauper.

Another first ascent on the North Pillar. A more direct climb that follows a more natural line, but still finishes up the Lauper. Toni Hiebeler, F. Maschke, Reinhold and Günther Messner.

1969 First ascent Japanese Summer Direct. A large Japanese team pushed up the Rote Fluh to the right of the 1938 line with fixed ropes in sixteen days.

First winter ascent of the Japanese Direct. Hans Peter Trachsel, Otto von Allmen, Hans Mueller, Peter Jürgen and Max Doerfliger.

1970 First ascent of the North Pillar Direct. Ian MacEacheran, Kenny Spence and Bugs McKeith. This climb still finished up the Lauper!

1976 First ascent of the Czech Pillar. Jiri Schmid, J. Rybica, Sylvia Kysilkova and P. Platesky. Another route to climb the Rote Fluh.

1977 First alpine-style ascent of the Harlin. Tobin Sorenson and Alex MacIntyre.

1978 First winter solo 1938 route. Tuneo Hasegawa.

First ascent of the Czech Winter Route. To the left of the Harlin. Jaroslav Flejberk, Josef Rybicka, Jiri Schmid and Miroslav Smid.

1980 First big wall rock route up the Pillar to the right of Rote Fluh, Les Portes du Chaos. Michel Piola and Gerard Hopfgartner.

1981 First rock climb for rock climbers' sake, North Corner. Hans and Cristel Howald. The obvious corner on the far right.

1983 First hard modern aid route, Geneva Pillar. Michel Piola and René Ghilini.

THE PIZ BADILE (3308m)

1867 The first ascent. W.A.B. Coolidge with François and Henri Dévouassoud.

1923 The first ascent of the North Ridge. Walter Risch and Alfred Zürcher.

1934 The first attempts on the North Face. Mario Molteni plus various partners.

1937 The first ascent of the North Face. Riccardo Cassin, Gino Esposito, Vittorio Ratti, Mario Molteni and Giuseppe Valsecchi. After topping out in a fierce storm, Molteni and Valsecchi died on the descent. 'A great climb marred by tragedy,' commented Riccardo Cassin.

1952 The first solo ascent of the Cassin route. Hermann Buhl. Buhl cycled in from Landeck and took four hours thirty minutes for his climb. The climbing world was stunned with admiration for this super climber.

1955 The first winter ascent of the North Ridge. Casimiro Ferrari, Aldo Anghileri and Giuseppe Negri.

1968 The first winter ascent of the Cassin route on the North Face. Paolo Armando, Camille Bournissen, Gianni Calcagno, Michel Darbellay, Alessandro Gogna and Daniel Troillet. They used fixed ropes, went home for Christmas and employed helicopters. What a contrast to the style of the first ascent.

1969 The first all women ascent of the Cassin on the North Face. Loulou Boulaz and Yvette Vaucher.

1978 The first two of many free climbs on excellent rock. Igor Koller and S. Silhan. A talented team.

THE DRU (3754m)

The Dru has two tops. The Grand Dru (3754m) separated from the Petit Dru (3733m) by a small gap, the Brèche des Drus.

1878   First ascent of the Grand Dru. Clinton T. Dent, J. Walker Hartley with Alexander Burgener and Kasper Maurer.

1879   First ascent of the Petit Dru. J Charlet-Straton, P. Payot and E. Folliguet.

1903   First traverse from the Petit to the Grand. E. Giraud with J. Ravanel and A. Comte.

1904   First attempt on the North Face. V.J.E. Ryan with Franz and Joseph Lochmatter.

1928   First winter ascent and traverse of both summits. Armand Charlet and C. Dévouassoud.

1932   First *descent* of the North Face. André Roch and Robert Gréloz abseiled the face. They used and carried 260m of rope and placed eight pitons. They declared the face unclimbable.

1935   The Swiss Raymond Lambert, M. Dupont, G. Gotch and R. Mussard reached the Niche.

      The first ascent of the North Face. Pierre Allain and Raymond Leininger. They assisted the Swiss descent and then finished the climb in fine style.

1952   New climb on the North Face. Henri and Pierre Leseur climbed from just left of the Allain start, traversed diagonally leftwards to finish on top of the Grand Dru. A masterpiece of route-finding and a great unsung climb that has been conveniently forgotten due to the attention lavished on the sunny western faces.

1964 First winter ascent of the North Face and Allain/ Leininger route. Gérard Dévouassoud, Yvon Masino and George Payot.

1970 First solo ascent of the North Face and Allain/Leininger route. Joel Coqueugnist.

1973 First new climb in winter on the North Face. Guides' route which starts as the Allain but climbs direct to the Niche and then left to gain the summit line. Yannick Seigneur, Michel Feuillarade, Claude Jager and Jean-Paul Paris.

1979 New climb on the North Face. A major rock climb from left to right, which has almost been forgotten. Patrick Berhault, Claude and Yves Remy.

1983 A huge rockfall from just below the summit spills tons of rock down the North Face. The noise was clearly heard down the valley in Chamonix.

First winter ascent of Leseur route. Thierry Renault and Andy Parkin.

1987 First solo ascent of Guides' route. Michel Duteurtre.

CIMA GRANDE DI LAVAREDO (2999m)

1869 First ascent of the mountain. Paul Grohmann with P. Salcher and E. Innerkofler. Now the descent route on the South Face.

1881 New climb on the South Face. Michel Innerkofler and Louis Tambosi.

1897 New climb on the East Face. J.S. Phillimore, A.G.S. Raynor with Antonio Dimai and Giuseppe Colli.

1908 New climb on the North-East Ridge. The first exposed space-walking climb! Angelo Dibona and Emil Stübler.

1913 New climb on the West Face. Hans Dülfer, Walter von Bernuth.

1929 New climb on the North-West Ridge. Ludwig Hall, Fritz Schütt and Walter Stösser.

1930–1 Attempts on the steep and forbidding North Face. Hans Steger and C. Carlesso, Emilio Comici and Renata Zanutti. Comici left a white handkerchief to mark his highest point.

1932 The first ascent of the North Face. Emilio Comici, Angelo and Giuseppe Dimai.

1934 The first solo ascent of the North Face. Emilio Comici solo climbed the line of his first ascent in three and a half hours.

1938 The first winter ascent of the North Face by the Comici route. Fritz Kasparek and Sepp Brunhuber as part of Kasparek's build up to his attempt on the unclimbed Eiger Nordwand.

1943 The first ascent of the North Face and Comici route by a woman. Elda Bianchini and Guiseppe Dimai.

1958 A new climb on the North Face which took a relatively direct line up the centre, the Brandler-Hasse route. Lothar Brandler, Dieter Hasse, Siegfried Löw and Jörg Lehne.

1963 The first ascent of the North Face by the Super Direct up the blank rock between the Comici and the Brandler-Hasse routes and in winter. Peter Siegert, Rainer Kauschke and Gerd Uhner. The ease of access enabled this sixteen-day climb to be staged as a media event, with live TV coverage.

1967 The blank rock left of the Brandler-Hasse route was bolted into submission. Why? Enrico Mauro and Mirko Minuzzo.

1978 The Comici climb, without using any artificial aids, just using natural rock holds. Jean-Claude Droyer and Yves Tugaye. The way forward to the super classic climbs in perfect natural style.

1982 The Brandler-Hasse route climbed in perfect natural style. Heinz Mariacher et al.

III

EQUIPMENT AND SUPPLIES

Our entire world consisted of Perkins and his seventeen blue plastic barrels. These fitted on his safari-style roof rack leaving enough space to lash down Tom and Kate's sledges, trolley and tractor.

No. 1:

5 cartons orange juice
8 tins tuna
2 tins tomatoes
1 packet small easter eggs
1 packet porridge oats
1 jar coffee
1 jar Marmite
1 jar salad cream
1 jar tomato ketchup
1 bag sugar
2 tea towels
2 blocks household soap
1 packet wheat bisks
12 packets Merothel

4 tins sardines
1 box tea bags
1 bag unmade popcorn
12 boxes tampons
1 bottle vegetable oil
2 packets sweet biscuits
2 packets cheese biscuits
2 Grandma's fruit cakes
1 bag plain flour
2 boxes sugar lumps
2 tubs face cream
12 packets Merocets
clothes pegs and line

No. 2:

2 washing-up bowls
3 dixies and lids
2 balls
2 dishcloths
1 roll cooking foil
1 packet washing powder
2 Granger's Zipease
1 Granger's SuperPel

2 Granger's G. Wax
2 Granger's Map Dry
2 Granger's G. Cream
1 aluminium kettle
1 Frog tower stove
1 Gaz stove
9 MSR fuel bottles
1 Pre-Mac Travel Well

1 bottle washing-up liquid
6 Granger's G. Wash
4 Granger's G. Clean

2 Granger's G. Sport
4 Granger's Nyloprufe
2 Granger's Superpruf

No. 3:

1 3-man mountain tent
1 4-man mountain tent
1 2-man mountain tent
1 1-man mountain tent
1 double Gore-Tex bivvi bag

1 bag sun creams and lipsalves
1 non-stick frying pan
1 Vapour Barrier sleeping-bag
  liner

No. 4:

4 pairs Brasher boots
3 pairs wellington boots
assorted Polisox socks
2 pairs child's après boots

5 pairs Reebok
3 pairs plastic sandals
2 pairs Rockport shoes

No. 5:

5 Gator neoprene face masks
2 Gator headbands
1 Gator neck garter
Sprayway Gore-Tex:
Osprey overtrousers
Duro overtrousers
Torridon jacket
Williwaw smock
Sprayway Malden Fleece:
2 jerseys
2 johns
Classic jacket

3 Gator neoprene sox
1 Gator bottle cover

2 Durable Design overmitts
5 Durable Design fleece gloves
assorted hats

2 Origin T
headband and neck gaiter

No. 6:

2 bath towels
3 single sheets
3 face flannels
1 4 Season sleeping bag
miscellaneous toiletries
2 double sheets

3 pillow cases
16 toilet rolls
1 box candles
1 plastic measuring jug
6 Prevent insect sprays

No. 7:

1 Thermarest	48 blocks chalk
5 chalkbags	1 pair Asolo La Rage
1 Soloist	1 pair Asolo SL1
1 chest harness	1 haul bag
25 quick draws	1 medium rucksac
50 karabiners	1 daysac

No. 8:

nappies	1 belay seat
waist bags	3 climbing harnesses
Elastoplast	3 tape étriers
2 daisy chains	20 long slings
OM1 camera and lenses	assorted straps
35 mm films	

No. 9:

3 pairs gaiters	3 rope bags
2 pairs Asolo plastic boots	

Cairngorm Ropes:

2 11 mm × 50 m	4 9 mm × 50 m

No. 10:

Scarface crampons	1 pair Cassin Antares
Switchblade crampons	1 pair Black Diamond Black
15 ice pegs	Prophet
30 rock pegs	1 pair Jumars
10 screw gate karabiners	1 pair crampons
4 ice tools and sparepicks	

No. 11:

15 pairs Polisox socks	2 towels

Children's clothes:

pants Kate:8 Tom:3	cardigans K:2
pyjamas K:3 T:2	3 fleece hats
trousers K:9 T:6	2 fleece trousers
rollnecks K:4 T:5	2 fleece jackets
shorts K:3 T:4	2 balaclavas
jumpers K:6 T:5	2 headbands
sweat shirts K:2 T:1	4 pairs gloves/mitts

No. 12:

6 Reebok tee shirts
3 Reebok sweat shirts
6 pairs running socks
2 Silking rollneck underwear
2 Silking long johns
2 Silking balaclavas
3 Silking gloves

3 Durable Design mitts
16 pairs Durable Design
    polarfleece gloves
hankies
knickers
8 Monberry rollnecks Profor

No. 13:

Sprayway Gore-Tex:
2 Duro overtrousers
1 Alto
1 Lady Cheyenne TL
1 Lady Spectrum
Sprayway Fleece:
Classic jacket
2 Origin T
1 Jammer
3 Johns
1 Zipper
Sprayway miscellaneous:
2 Zest
hats
balaclavas

1 Cat's Paw
1 Williwaw
1 Lady Torridon
1 Osprey overtrousers

1 Workout
3 jerseys
1 Farmer John
1 pair Tites

mitts
headbands
neck gaiters

No. 14:
swimming costumes
Strappal hand and finger tape

2 down quilts and covers
3 head torches

No. 15/16/17:
THIS FOOD FITTED INTO THREE
    VERY HEAVY BARRELS:
540 Jordan's cereal bars –
    Original, Oatbran and Frusli

Haldane vegetarian food:
48 packets Sosmix – cheese/
    onion, country herb and
    original

36 packets Burgamix – original
    and onion/chive
6 packets Hera Vegetable
    Casserole

6 packets Hera Vegetable Curry
6 packets Hera Vegetable Chilli
6 packets Hera Vegetable Stroganov
10 packets Hera Tomato Soup mix
12 packets Amazing Grain Cereal Savoury
6 packets Amazing Grain Savoury Couscous
6 packets Amazing Grain Sultan's Pilaf
6 packets Amazing Grain Savoury Paella
48 packets Realeat Vegeburger – herb and spicy
12 tins Granose Bolognaise
12 (400 g) tubs Ovaltine
42 tubs Isostar powder
1 case Tracker chocolate bars

IV

SPONSORS AND SUPPLIERS

The Big Six would not have turned into *A Hard Day's Summer* without the kindness and generosity of the following companies. Three cheers from the whole family for your support!

AGROPHARM
Buckingham House
Church Road
Penn
High Wycombe
HP10 8LN
England

Prevent insect spray suitable
for use on children

ANIMAL LTD
Sir Peter Thompson House
Market Close
Poole
Dorset
BH15 1NE
England
Ian Elliot

Wild Watch Straps

**BLACK DIAMOND
EQUIPMENT LTD**
2084 East 3900 South
Salt Lake City
UT 84124
USA
Mariah Cranor

Black Prophet ice tools, Alaska
picks, Switch Blade crampons

**BRASHER BOOT COMPANY
LTD**
White Cross
Lancaster
LA1 4XY
England
Chris Brasher and Alison Helme

Hillmaster and Fellmaster walking boots

BRITAX-EXCELSIOR LTD
Churchill Way West
Andover
Hampshire
FP10 3UW
England
Alan Thornton

Mountain bike helmets for children and adults, specialist mountain bike child seats

CAIRNGORM CLIMBING ROPE CO. LTD
Newtonmore
Inverness-shire
PH20 1DL
Scotland
Amanda Mackintosh

Kestrel, Eagle, Osprey, Raven and Thunderbird climbing ropes

COLMANS OF NORWICH plc
Carrow
Norwich
NR1 2DD
England
Norma Walker

Apple and blackcurrant juice

COYOTE MOUNTAIN BIKES (UK) LTD
P.O. Box 14
Gosforth
Newcastle-upon-Tyne
NE13 7YZ
England
Steve Fenton

Coyote Pro 4 mountain bike

DURABLE DESIGNS
P.O. Box 130
RT 16/302
Intervale
NH 0385 0130
USA
Cort Hansen and Rob Nadler

Polartec microfibre inner gloves, Polartec gloves, fleece gloves and Expedition overmitts

ELMWOOD DESIGNS LTD
Ghyll Road
Guiseley
Leeds
LS20 9LT
England
Michael Owen

Design work for Sprayway

FRONT PAGE CREATIONS
6A Kenton Park Shopping
Centre
Gosforth
Newcastle-upon-Tyne
NE3 4NN
England
Carlton Reid

Public relations for Sprayway Ltd and advice on mountain bike/access

GATOR SPORTS INC.
510 West 3560 South
Salt Lake City
UT 84115
USA
Connie Gardner

Neoprene face masks, ears, bottle covers, sox

GRANGERS INTERNATIONAL LTD
Grange Close
Clover Nook Industrial Park
Alfreton
DE55 4QT
England
Tim Wilson

Zipease, Weltseal, G. Wax, G. Wash, G. Cream, G. Sport, Mapdry, Nylopruf, Superpruf, G. Clean, Superpel

GRIVEL
11013
Courmayeur AO
Italy
Gioachine Gobbi

Mont Blanc and Rambo crampons, Face Nord and Goulotte picks, Evolution ice tools and adjustable ski poles

HALDANE FOOD GROUP plc
Howard Way
Newport Pagnell
Buckinghamshire
MK16 9PY
England
Alex Crozier

Vegetarian food: Sosmix, Burgamix, Vegeburger, Direct Foods, Hera Meals, Amazing Grains, Realeat, Granose

W. JORDAN (CEREALS) LTD
Holme Mills
Biggleswade
Bedfordshire
SG18 9JX
England
Bill Jordan and Amanda Hill

Cereal bars: Original, Oatbran and Frusli

MARION MERRELL DOW LTD
Lakeside House
Stockley Park
Uxbridge
UB11 1BE
England
Maire O'Reilly

Merocets and Merothel throat and nose care

MARS (UK) LTD
Dundee Road
Slough
SL1 4LG
England
Julie Will

Tracker chocolate bars

MONTBERRY LTD
416 Main Street
Countisthorpe
Leicester
LE8 3QX
England

Roger Pemberton and Jim Myer

Profor cotton rollnecks

MOUNTAIN SAFETY RESEARCH INC.
P.O. Box 24547
4225 Second Avenue South
Seattle
WA 98124
USA
Shanna Waters
Fuel bottles, XGK11 and Expedition stoves, Expedition pan sets

NEVISRANGE plc
Torlundy
Fort William
TH33 6SW
Scotland
Spike, Cally, Alison and Debbie

Public relations and skiing

ORION EQUIPMENT LTD
261 Sauchiehall Street
Glasgow
G2 3EZ
Scotland
Ian Sykes

Cassin climbing helmets, Antares ice tools, Scarface and Classic crampons

POLISOX LTD
Park Road
Blaby
Leicester
LE8 3ED
England
Charles Polito and Mark O'Shaughnessy

Bear children's ski tubes, Ski Tubes, Davos, Tignes, Steamboat and Baseline socks and Polypro liners

PRE-MAC KENT LTD
40 Holden Park Road
Southborough
Tunbridge Wells
Kent
TN4 OER
England
Ray Higham

Travel Well filters and bottles for pure water

RAGGED MOUNTAIN EQUIPMENT INC.
P.O. Box 130
RT 16/302
Intervale
NH 0385 0130
USA
Rob Nadler and Cort Hansen

Tee shirts

REEBOK (UK) LTD
Moor Lane Mill
Lancaster
LA1 1GF
England
John Disley, Jan Corbett and Shirley Brown

Complete family outfitted in athletic clothing and running shoes

ROCKPORT CO LTD
Mill 2
Moor Lane
Lancaster
LA1 1GF
England
Linda Humphries

Prowalker shoes, Outdoor leisure boots

ROLEX WATCH COMPANY LTD
3 Stratford Place
London
W1N OER
England
John Hunt

Lady Date wrist chronometer

SILKING LTD
5 Lancer House
Hussar Court
Westside View
Waterlooville
PO7 7SE
England
Peter Collett

Silk rollnecks, long johns, balaclavas, gloves and scarves

SMITH & NEPHEW MEDICAL LTD
101 Hessle Road
Hull
HU3 2BN
England
Alison Brown

Elastoplast, Strappal tape

SPRAYWAY LTD
16 Chester Street
Manchester
M1 5GE
England
John Hunt

Waterproof Gore-Tex jackets
and overtrousers, Polartec 100
tops and bottoms, Polartec 200
and Polartec 300 jackets, Hard-
rock children's jackets and wind-
breaks, Sprayway Additions
head-bands, hats, mitts and balaclavas.

**VENTURA HOLDINGS (UK)
LTD**
Hall House
New Hutton
Kendal
LA8 OAH
England
Gordon Fraser and Mark Dig-
gins

Asolo Alpine plastic boots and
rock shoes

**VUARNET/MOUNTAIN
LEISURE LTD**
Fovant Mews
12A Noyna Road
London
SW17 7PH
England
John Ferguson

Mountain bike glasses, Alpine
glasses and goggles

WANDER LTD
Station Road
King's Langley
Hertfordshire
WD4 8LJ
England
Wendy Gornicki

Ovaltine and Isostar drinks, tee
shirts and sweat shirts

YORKSHIRE BANK plc
14 High Street
Alfreton
DE5 7BB
England
Martin Johnson

Advice and expedition bankers

V

GLOSSARY

ABSEIL

A quick method of descent. A double rope is hung down from a secure point of attachment and the climber makes a controlled slide down it. The rope is then pulled down by pulling one end to be used again. Also known as rappeling.

ACCLIMATISATION

The human body has to adapt to the rarefied air of altitude. Some people acclimatise more easily than others. The ultimate penalty at high altitudes for not being properly acclimatised can be death.

ALP

The high summer grass and pasture above the valley, but below the snowline.

ALPINE CLUB

The world's first climbing club, founded in 1857 in London.

ANCHOR

A point of attachment to the mountain, for the rope or climber.

ARETE

A sharp, narrow rock or ice ridge.

BELAYING

Fastening into an anchor to safeguard a moving climber/climbers.

BERGSCHRUND

A crevasse or gap between the glacier and the mountain.

BIVOUAC

A night spent out without benefit of a prepared camp.

BOLTS

Where no natural cracks or fissures occur, a hole is drilled and an expansion or chemical bolt installed.

BRIDGING
Climbing wide chimneys by straddling one foot and one hand on each wall.

CAMS/CAMMING
Complicated mechanical devices that provide secure anchors in natural rock cracks and fissures.

CARABINER
see KARABINER

CHALK
Magnesium carbonate in either block or powder form. Used to keep the rock climber's hands sweat-free. Carried in a chalk bag fastened around the climber's waist.

CHIMNEY
A wide crack, sometimes large enough for the climber to climb on the inside.

CHOCKSTONE
A boulder or block jammed in a crack, chimney or gully.

COL
A dip or depression in a ridge, usually between two peaks.

CORNICE
A snow lip projecting over the edge of a ridge, gully or face.

COULOIR
French for a gully.

CRAMPONS
A framework of alloy steel spikes which fit over the sole of a boot. Used for climbing snow and ice.

CREVASSE
A crack or fissure in the surface of a glacier.

DAISY CHAIN
A long sling made of tape webbing stitched into small karabiner-sized pockets, so that the length can be easily adjusted, *see* SLING.

DESCENDEUR
An alloy device to make abseils controlled and easier.

FROSTBITE

Caused by ice crystals forming between the cells with constriction of minor blood vessels. This leads to a reduction in the oxygen supply to the cells and they then deteriorate and can become infected.

GENDARME

A pinnacle on a ridge.

GLACIER

A slow-flowing river of ice.

GROOVE

A shallow open fissure.

GULLY

A wide fissure in the side of a mountain, *see* COULOIR.

HARNESS

Made of nylon tape, to which the rope is attached.

ICE AXE

Modern axes are made of an alloy or fibre composite shaft with a spike at its base and are topped with a pick and adze.

ICE SCREWS

Pitons for driving or screwing into ice.

ICE TOOLS

Specialist ice axes often used in pairs for climbing steep ice and frozen waterfalls. One usually has a hammer head instead of an adze.

JAM/JAMMING

Wedging a hand, finger or foot in a crack or fissure.

KARABINER

An oval or dee-shaped alloy metal ring, one side of which opens and is spring-loaded, used to attach ropes, slings or harness (also called biners, krabs).

LAYBACK/LIEBACK

Where hands and feet are used in opposition, classically to climb a corner crack.

LINE

The route followed up a mountain feature.

MANTELSHELF
An awkward climbing movement that involves pressing down on a ledge or feature with your hands until you can get your feet on to it!

MIXED GROUND/CLIMBING
Climbing which varies between rock, snow and ice.

MORAINE
Large banks of earth and stones pushed up by a glacier.

NUTS
Sophisticated alloy wedges mounted on short wire loops of different sizes that can be wedged into natural constrictions in cracks and fissures to form anchors.

PILLAR
A narrow column of rock which juts out from the parent mountain.

PITCH
The distance between two anchors, ideally a full rope-length of 45–55 metres.

PITON
Metal spikes of different shapes that can be hammered into natural cracks and fissures to provide anchors. Also known as pegs or pins, *see* ICE SCREWS.

QUICKDRAWS
Short tape slings with a karabiner at either end to extend a belay.

RIB
A small ridge.

RIDGE
The crest where two opposing mountain faces join.

SCREE
A slope of small loose stones.

SERAC
An ice pinnacle.

SLING
A loop of rope or tape webbing used to attach climber, harness, belay.

A Hard Day's Summer

SOLOIST
An American-designed and manufactured device that automatically locks the rope threaded through it in the event of a fall, and so enables a solo climber to be protected by a rope without the need for another climber to belay.

SPINDRIFT
Light powder snow blown about by the wind.

STANCE
A place the climber can rest and belay.

VERGLAS
A very thin layer of ice formed on rock.

155

VI

BIBLIOGRAPHY

Readers who have got this far may like to continue the tragic and fascinating story of the Big Six.

ALLAIN, Pierre, *Alpinisme et Compétition*
BIRKETT, Bill & PEASCOD, Bill, *Women Climbing*, London, 1989
BONATTI, Walter, *On the Heights*, London, 1979
                The Great Days, London, 1974
BONINGTON, Chris, *I Chose to Climb*, London, 1966, 1985
                The Next Horizon, London, 1973, 1986
                Mountaineer, London, 1989
BUHL, Hermann, *Nanga Parbat Pilgrimage*, London, 1981
CASSIN, Riccardo *50 Years of Alpinism*, London, 1981
CLEARE, John, *Mountains*, London, 1975
DESMAISON, René, *Total Alpinism*, London, 1982
DIEMBERGER, Kurt, *Summits and Secrets*, London, 1971, 1991
ENGEL, Claire, *Mountaineering in the Alps*, London, 1971
GERVASUTTI, Giusto, *Gervasutti's Climbs*, London, 1957, 1978
HARRER, Heinrich, *The White Spider*, London, 1959, 1983
HASTON, Dougal, *The Eiger*, London, 1974
HASTON, Dougal and GILLMAN, Peter, *Eiger Direct*, London, 1966
HECKMAIR, Anderl, *My Life as a Mountaineer*, London, 1975
HIEBELER, Toni, *The North Face in Winter*, 1962
MAGNONE, Guido, *The West Face*, London, 1955
MAZEAUD, Pierre, *Naked Before the Mountains*, London, 1974
MESSNER, Reinhold, *The Seventh Grade*, London, 1974
                The Big Walls, London, 1978
MILNE, Malcolm, *The Book of Modern Mountaineering*, London 1968
OLSEN, Jack, *The Climb up to Hell*, 1962
PATEY, Tom, *One Man's Mountains*, London, 1971, 1986
RÉBUFFAT, Gaston, *Men and the Matterhorn*, 1967
                Starlight and Storm, London, 1969

ROBERTS, Eric, *Welzenbach's Climbs*, London, 1980

ROCH, André, *Climbs of my Youth*, London, 1949

ROTH, Arthur, *Eiger – Wall of Death*, London, 1982

SCOTT, Doug, *Big Wall Climbing*, London, 1974

TASKER, Joe, *Savage Arena*, London, 1982

TERRAY, Lionel, *Conquistadors of the Useless*, London, 1975

ULLMAN, James Ramsey, *Straight Up*, New York, 1968

VAUSE, Mikel, *Rock and Roses*, La Crescenta, Calif., 1990

WHILLANS, Don and ORMEROD, Alick, *Portrait of a Mountaineer*, London, 1971, 1973

WILLIAMS, Cicely, *Women on the Rope*, London, 1973

WILSON, Ken, *The Games Climbers Play*, London, 1978

ANDREW McCLOY

LAND'S END TO JOHN O'GROATS

A CHOICE OF FOOTPATHS FOR WALKING THE
LENGTH OF BRITAIN

- The ultimate walking challenge for end-to-enders or to
  enjoy piecemeal
- By coastal paths and mountain tracks, tow paths and
  abandoned railways, drove roads and unfrequented
  country lanes
- Three individual routes the length of Britain
- With up-to-date information on the status of our vast
  footpath heritage

CORONET BOOKS

**CHRIS BONINGTON AND
ROBIN KNOX-JOHNSTON**

SEA, ICE & ROCK

Chris Bonington goes sailing.
Robin Knox-Johnston goes climbing.

Chris Bonington may have climbed just about everything up to and including Everest but when it comes to sailing, he is, frankly, all at sea.
Robin Knox-Johnston may have sailed round the world single-handed but his climbing experience is strictly restricted to clambering up and down masts.
So how would each fare in a skill-swapping expedition? And nothing easy either. A voyage to the ice-bound Greenland coast, followed by a trek across a glacial wilderness to an unclimbed granite and ice peak.

'Intoxicating stuff revealing bravery, skill, courage, fear, intelligence – everything' *The Guardian*

CORONET BOOKS

WALT UNSWORTH

ENCYCLOPAEDIA OF MOUNTAINEERING

Personalities, peaks, climbing techniques, potted histories of ranges, the ethics, the jargon, the gear – since 1975 the *Encyclopaedia of Mountaineering* has been an unrivalled and much thumbed source of every aspect of climbing knowledge, from the Abraham brothers to Andrzej Zawada, from Alpine guides to competition climbing, alpenstocks to quickdraws.

This new illustrated edition has been expanded by almost a third, reorganised and updated. Its 400 plus climber entries include a greatly strengthened representation from Europe and the USA and its statistics cover first ascents and the highest mountains in all the major and many of the lesser known climbing areas of the world.

WALT UNSWORTH is a former editor of *Climber and Rambler* and editorial director of Cicerone Press. His books include *Everest*, *Savage Snows*, *the story of Mont Blanc* and *Hold the Heights: the foundations of mountaineering*.

CORONET BOOKS